P9-CFE-669

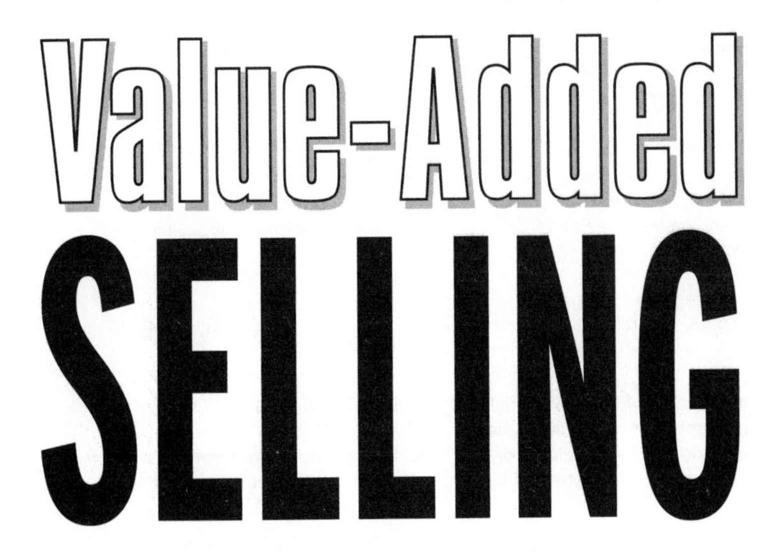

How to Sell More
Profitably, Confidently, and
Professionally by Competing
on VALUE, Not Price

TOM REILLY

McGraw-Hill

New York Chicago San Francisco Lisbon London Madrid Mexico City
Milan New Delhi San Juan Seoul Singapore Sydney Toronto

The McGraw-Hill Companies

Library of Congress Cataloging-in-Publication Data

Reilly, Thomas P.
Value-added selling : how to sell more profitably, confidently, and professionally by competing on value, not price / Tom Reilly.
p. cm.
Rev. ed. of: Value-added selling techniques. c1989.
Includes index.
ISBN 0-07-140881-9
1. Selling. 2. Value-added. I. Reilly, Thomas P. Value-added selling techniques. II. Title.

HF5438.25 .R45 2003
658.85—dc21 2002029359

1 2 3 4 5 6 7 8 9 0 DOC/DOC 1 0 9 8 7 6 5 4 3 2

ISBN 0-07-140881-9

This book is printed on acid-free paper.

To my parents, John and Mossie Reilly, whose unconditional love and encouragement sparked in me the desire to dream beyond the obvious and the courage to chase these dreams

CONTENTS

PART III VALUE-ADDED SELLING TACTICS 129

PART IV VALUE-ADDED SELLING—SPECIAL TOPICS 203

ACKNOWLEDGMENTS

I WANT TO thank these people who have proved that *we* is greater than *me*: Julie Heyer, a writing coach, whose input added value to this manuscript; my staff, Linda and Joann, who have read and reread this manuscript and offered their ideas, which generally challenged my ideas; Charlotte, my wife, whose editing skills are legendary in our company; Danielle Egan-Miller, my editor at McGraw-Hill, whose faith in this project was inspiring; and all of the other folks at McGraw-Hill whose input made this manuscript a quality book.

INTRODUCTION

CONGRATULATIONS! YOU'RE DOING something that fewer than 10 percent of your peers do—you're reading a book on your profession. You're demonstrating a common characteristic of successful people: personal initiative, which is all that stuff you do without someone's telling you that you must do it. Initiative is your internal kick-starter. Motivation is a do-it-to-yourself-for-yourself kind of thing, and you are motivated. I can tell.

Customers want to deal with motivated, knowledgeable salespeople. This means investing in your personal research and development, since the product or brand over which you have the most control is you. I call this "Brand-You." The way to build your knowledge base is by reading and studying. Sir Francis Bacon wrote, "Knowledge is power." If that's true, what you don't know holds great power over you. Reading this book is self-empowerment. Again, congratulations.

Thank you for giving me the opportunity to share with you the power of Value-Added Selling. I'm passionate about this message, which you'll see as we get deeper into this book. Value-Added Selling is a content-rich message of hope. It's a message that says you can compete profitably without cutting your price, even in the most price-sensitive environment. You accomplish this by selling your total value-added solution.

My journey down this path began in 1981 when I sold my business in Houston to pursue a full-time speaking career. At first, I spent most of my time conducting five-day public selling seminars. I soon amassed a list of objections that salespeople brought to these seminars, and guess what was consistently number one on this list? Price.

Everyone had encountered the same problem: "Your price is too high." "It's not in the budget." "Your competition offered us a better deal." "I must put this out for bid." "That's more than I want to spend." How many of these sound familiar to you?

That prompted me to write my first book, *Value-Added Selling Techniques*. At the time, I had no idea it would help spawn a global movement called Value-Added Selling. Since then, I've spent about 90 percent of my speaking-and-training time teaching salespeople, their managers, and their customer service representatives the Value-Added Selling philosophy.

I'm thrilled to be able to share this new edition of *Value-Added Selling* with you. Since my pioneering work in this area began, I've had the privilege of working with some of the best organizations in the world, global leaders in their industries. I was their student as often as I was their teacher. This new edition of *Value-Added Selling* shows you some of what I've learned on my journey from the time the first edition of this book was published.

My selling roots are in the chemical industry. It was my first real sales job. The chemical business is a commodity industry. When I worked for a large manufacturer, we private-labeled products for our competitors. They sold our stuff under their label. Likewise, when I owned a distributorship, we sold the exact same products as six other distributors in town. There was no product differentiation; we could sell only the unique value that our company and people represented. The commodity mind-set exists in many industries today.

At the same time, other forces are creating urgency for Value-Added Selling. The competition is fierce. Superstores, armed with discount prices and less-than-super service, are reshaping the competitive landscape in retail. Integrated supply and group purchasing organizations are redefining industrial selling. And the advent of E-tailing (selling on the Internet) has everyone looking into his or her marketing crystal ball. The race is on.

Today's buyers are more knowledgeable, have greater access to supply alternatives, and demand more from suppliers. Buyers want more for less. Quality, once the bastion of a select few, has now become first-cut criteria for all suppliers. If you don't offer good quality, you don't get a chance to compete. Buyers don't want to talk to you.

In *Value-Added Selling*, I want to share ideas and insights that will help you to deliver more value to your customers and to compete at a higher level than your competition. You'll discover that the Value-Added Selling philosophy is a customer-focused approach to business. Value-added sellers are committed to equity in their relationships and addicted to excellence in their performance.

I want to teach you to think as customers think, to define value in their terms, and to present a compelling nonprice argument for why the customer should choose your alternative over the competition.

I want to help you to get credit for all the value added that your company brings to the table, encourage you to continue to re-create value for the customer, and show you how to increase customer retention and loyalty via increased customer satisfaction. The bottom line is that I want to help you sell more products, more profitably, to more people.

To achieve this, I've organized *Value-Added Selling* into four parts. Part I introduces you to the Value-Added Selling philosophy and provides you with valuable insight into what customers really want from suppliers. I share with you inside data from my 10,000-piece survey on buyer preferences. Part I answers the question, "Why should I embrace the Value-Added Selling philosophy?"

Part II is the strategic side of Value-Added Selling. You learn that value-added salespeople use eleven strategies to outsell the competition. This part answers the question, "What should I do to sell our value-added solution?"

Part III is the tactical side of Value-Added Selling. Here, you learn the steps of the value-added sales call: how to prepare, execute, and evaluate your selling activities. This part answers the question, "How do I make the value-added sales call?"

Part IV is a bonus part—true value added. In this part, I discuss additional topics for value-added salespeople: selling to high-level decision makers, the impact of technology on sales, how to use sales letters, and value-added time management.

I encourage you to read with highlighters and an open mind. You'll need both to draw the most from this book. Commit to using these Value-Added Selling ideas. Commitment is the degree to which you will inconvenience yourself for something. You have already taken a step on the commitment path by purchasing *Value-Added Selling*. Walk down this path daily by using what you learn in this book, and it will make a significant difference for you. *Value-Added Selling* will help you reach the next level in your career.

Good luck.

PART I

VALUE-ADDED SELLING PHILOSOPHY

IN PART I, I introduce you to the Value-Added Selling philosophy. Many people tell me that they like the Value-Added Selling philosophy because it parallels their personal business philosophies. Value-Added Selling is a customer-first and customer-oriented philosophy. We put the customer at the center of what we do. This translates into the customer-value focus to which I refer throughout the book.

In Chapter 1, I describe how value-added organizations compete—with their people. A value-added organization believes that its employees represent the single unique dimension of value. Organizational excellence is the natural outcome of individual and team excellence. How you approach your career, interact with your peers, and interface with your customers determines the level at which your company competes.

In Chapter 2, I explain value added and discuss what buyers really want from sellers. They want more than a cheap price. They want a positive total experience with your solution. I also discuss the impact of discounting on your company and the consequences of using a price-only selling strategy.

In Chapter 3, I introduce you to the Value-Added Selling process. This model and your understanding of it serve as a foundation on which I build throughout the rest of the book. The Value-Added Selling process teaches you how to *think* about selling, not just to sell. This analytical skill is unique to Value-Added Selling and vital to your success.

In Chapter 4, I show you how to identify your company's value added. Passion sells, and enthusiasm is contagious. To be able to sell your value added, you must first know and understand your value added. This in-depth examination of your value added will light your fuse.

CHAPTER 1

THE VALUE-ADDED ORGANIZATION

WHAT MAKES GREAT organizations great? Is it their products? Is it their service? Is it their employees? Yes, yes, yes. They are great for all these reasons. Value-added organizations are great because they deliver a valuable *total* experience to their customers. That's what this chapter is about—how your company can become a value-added organization. The way you approach your career, the way you interact with your peers, and the way you interface with customers determine the level at which your company competes.

Specifically, this chapter has the following aims:

- Introduce you to the three ways organizations compete
- Describe the chief characteristics of value-added peak competitor organizations
- Discuss how you, interacting with your peers, determine how effectively your organization competes

The Three Styles of Competitors

Since 1981, I've had the privilege of working with some of the best organizations in the world—global leaders in their industries. I was their student as well as their teacher. I learned as much from them as I taught them. One of the lessons they taught me was how to compete in an industry.

Equalizers

At the most fundamental level of competitiveness are the equalizers, or qualifiers. They want to be as good as everyone else in their industries. They seek ways to close the gap between themselves and their competitors. Equalizers have a lot of catching up to do. They live the *me-too* philosophy.

If one competitor offers twenty-four-hour service, equalizers will copy this. If another competitor offers better quality, equalizers will attempt to close that gap. They are always seeking ways to level the playing field between themselves and everyone else. Their competitive focus is external. They take their cues from the competition and respond appropriately.

Differentiators

The differentiators represent the next higher level of competitors. They want to be better than the rest of the pack. They seek ways to expand the gap between themselves and everyone else in their industries.

Differentiators live the *and-then-some* philosophy. If one of their competitors offers forty-eight-hour turnaround time on orders, differentiators will try to do it in twenty-four hours. Like equalizers, differentiators take their lead from the competition. They have an external, competitive focus. Their goal is to be better than everyone else in the market.

Value-Added Peak Competitors

The highest-level competitors are value-added peak competitors. These value-added organizations (and people) march to a different drumbeat. They rarely focus on the gap between themselves and the competition. They concentrate on bridging the gap between potential and reality—their potential and the customer's reality.

Value-added peak competitors are those organizations and people who embrace and live the value-added philosophy. They expect the best from themselves, which enables them to maximize the value they bring to their customers.

Value-added peak competitors have a positive addiction to excellence—they're hooked on doing things well. They pursue excellence in all that they do. They've discovered the secret of companies that adopt a *business excellence* approach: they outperform the competition, create lasting value, and achieve long-term success in the process. The stock market performance of companies that practice *business excellence* beats the S&P 500 average return on investment by five to one.

There are no sacred cows in these value-added peak competitor organizations. They challenge the status quo with this question: "Does this policy, procedure, or process add value to our efforts, or does it just add cost?" Your company's practices that add cost without value diminish your position in the market. They slow you down. It's like driving with one foot on the brake and one foot on the accelerator.

The value-added way of life is a simple philosophy that permeates every aspect of your being: Do more of that which adds value to your life and less of that which adds little or no value—whether it's time management, career development, personal and professional relationships, or spiritual, emotional, and physical well-being.

Value-added peak competitors are proud of what they've accomplished but possess the humility to admit that they can still grow and get better. Couple this humility and pride with a curiosity about their own potential, and value-added peak competitors challenge themselves with this question: "Is this the best we can do with the resources we have available, or can we reach higher?"

Value-added peak competitors benchmark their accomplishments against their own company's potential, not against the rest of the market. They respect, but do not fear, the competition. They realize that their primary mission is to serve customers better, not just to beat the competition. They defeat competitors by serving customers better. Their focus is clear.

It is a customer-value focus that defines value and success in customer terms. It's not value until the customer calls it value. Value-added peak competitors view success as their ability to help their customers achieve higher levels of success. By helping customers become more successful, value-added peak competitors, in turn, experience success.

Value-added peak competitors focus more on making a difference than on just making a deal. They realize that if they work tenaciously to make a difference for their customers, they will have all the deals they can handle. And they make a difference with their employees.

For value-added peak competitors, people represent the single, unique dimension of value. Why? Because there's no commodity in creativity, and there's no traffic jam on the extra mile.

Organizational Excellence

Organizational excellence is the natural outcome of individual and team excellence. How employees approach their careers, how they interact with their peers, and how they engage customers affect the bottom line. Becoming a value-added organization is a top-down, bottom-up, and inside-out process. Everyone in your company must buy into this philosophy.

How You Approach Your Career

Whether you're the CEO, the vice president of sales, a mid-level manager, a customer service rep, a factory worker, or a salesperson, your performance affects your organization's performance. Are you a cost center or a profit center to your company? Do you add value or cost to your company's efforts? What are you doing to add value to your company's efforts?

Value-added peak competitor employees seek ways to add value because that's the way they live their lives. They naturally put forth extra effort. Excelling is a habit for them. One effective way to add value is to identify impact areas where you can make a difference for the customer and for your company. Your behavior and how you treat customers have a positive impact on your company's performance.

A few years ago, I was in Sacramento working with an equipment dealer. In an effort to identify impact areas, I assembled a group of employees and asked them, "How do you personally add value?"

One of the mechanics said, "On every piece of equipment that I service, I perform a five-point safety check just to be sure that everything leaving my repair bay is safe for our customers to operate."

One of the salespeople in the group heard this and asked, "Do you perform that test on everything?"

The mechanic said, "Yeah."

And the salesman responded, "I can sell that value added this afternoon."

Other employees in this company also found ways to add value. A manager added value by the amount of face time he spent with customers. He could get things done. By having his ear that close to the ground, he was able to prevent many of the fires that other companies fought. He was a real go-getter.

One salesperson added value with her twenty-four-hour accessibility to customers. She gave them her home phone number, beeper number, cell phone number, and inside company contacts. She made sure that her customers were never out of touch.

In the same vein, an accounting person understood her role as building bridges with customers to draw them in, not walls to keep the bums out. She looked for ways to help customers qualify—not disqualify—for credit.

A driver went the extra mile for his customers by adjusting his delivery route for his customers' convenience. "I want to make it easy for our customers to receive our deliveries. Other drivers won't do that," he said. This driver made it a habit to do what others viewed as a hassle. This positive addiction to excellence is what characterizes value-added peak competitors—*they make habitual what others consider to be a hassle*.

"What am I personally doing today to add value to our efforts?" If everyone in your organization asked and answered this question daily, I believe you could lift your organization to the next level, with your employees. After all, employees are the greatest source of value for companies.

How You Interact with Your Peers

Everyone in an organization has a customer—internal and/or external. External customers are those traditional customers outside your company who pay for your goods and services.

Internal customers are other employees in your company whom you serve. The service department is the internal customer of the parts department. Customer service is the internal customer of the sales department. Information technology serves marketing. Employees serve management, and vice versa. Human resources serves most other departments. Identifying your internal customers allows you to build customer satisfaction with them. Who are your internal customers?

Two corollaries follow this internal customer relationship. First, you can serve your external customers only to the degree to which you serve your internal customers. Second, everything you do to serve internal customers has an outward, rippling effect on your external customers.

Customer satisfaction mirrors employee satisfaction. Satisfied workers create satisfied customers. Loyal employees create loyal customers. Customer loyalty parallels employee loyalty, making loyalty a leading predictor of your company's profitability. Satisfied, loyal customers return and bring their friends, too.

Value-added organizations pride themselves on teamwork. They realize that a team is only as strong as its weakest member. They leverage this synergy to serve their customers better. Three traits characterize value-added teamwork.

First, "We is greater than me." Teams fail when there's too much "me" and not enough "we." Synergy is the collective effort of everyone on your team. Two people working jointly on a project bring more collective effort to the table than the sum total of their individual and independent efforts. As Jack Welch, the legendary CEO of GE, puts it, "None of us is even close to being as smart as all of us." This is synergy—*we* is greater than *me*.

Second, value-added peak competitors treat each other with the same respect they desire for their best customers. Employees who work together in an environment of mutual respect form a special dynamic that extends to the way they treat their external customers. A culture of respect develops.

Third, they build each other up, not break each other down. With all the competition you have on the streets, do you really need internal competition? Of course not. How you support fellow team members and how you serve internal customers affect your organization's performance. Remember, organizational excellence is the natural outcome of individual and team performance.

In some companies, one department may view other internal departments as competitors, not peers or teammates. One department feels the need to compete with another. An expression in management psychology vividly describes this phenomenon: the silo effect. One department acts as if it has walls surrounding and isolating it from other departments. It acts as if it were a separate company, often competing for in-house resources and credit.

How can you effectively fight a battle on the streets when you have several departments from the same company battling each other? The message you need to spread internally is: "We are not the enemy." Value-Added Selling is a team sport. The salesperson may sell the first item, but it's the customer's total experience with a company that brings him or her back.

How You Engage Customers

In value-added organizations, serving customers is a privilege, not a pain. Customer service is more than a department. It's a philosophy in which everyone in the organization feels—and acts—accountable for creating satisfied customers.

Value-added organizations are proactive with their service. They nip problems in the bud. They anticipate and act in advance. Being proactive means never having to apologize to the customer for poor service.

Because of their strong customer focus, value-added peak competitors define value in customer terms. Thus, customers will pay for the value with a higher selling price. If you define value in seller terms, you will pay for it with a higher discount.

Selling is relationship management. How well do you manage the relationship with your customers? Customer loyalty goes with the person, not with the brand. One of the great marketing myths is brand loyalty. While customers prefer brands, they reserve loyalty for people. This loyalty results from their total experience in dealing with a supplier. What kind of total experience do your customers have with your company? How is your customer loyalty? How is your repeat business?

Value-added organizations are constantly looking for ways to re-create value for their customers. A desperate curiosity about their own company's potential coupled with a strong customer-value focus encourages value-added organizations to dream and to stretch. They live by asking, "What if?"

"What if we could do it this way?" "What if we could design a better way for the customer to do things?" "What if we could make it easier for the customer to do business with us?"

Value-added organizations are great because of their people. They believe that people can and do make a difference. With the commoditization of products and the convergence of services, companies are churning out millions of look-alike products and services. The single, unique dimension of value is people.

A company president said to me recently, "Tom, we used to be a value-added peak competitor organization until we lost our best people. Now we're just like everyone else."

Value-Added Selling Review and Action Points

1. To become a value-added peak competitor, you must pursue excellence in all that you do, challenge the status quo, and judge your accomplishments by internal, not external, standards of performance.

2. Live the value-added philosophy by applying this simple yet powerful attitude to your daily activities: Do more of that which adds value to your life and less of that which adds little or no value to your life.
3. Organizational excellence is the natural outcome of individual and team excellence. How you approach your career, how you interact with your peers, and how you interface with customers determine the level at which your company competes.

CHAPTER 2

VALUE-ADDED SELLING

SINCE THE PUBLICATION of my first book on this topic, I've witnessed an explosion of look-alike products and services. I've met people who say they are doing Value-Added Selling, but they can't define it for me. I've talked to trainers who tell me they have their own value-added sales courses; generally, it's old wine in a new skin.

This chapter introduces you to the Value-Added Selling philosophy. In it, I build a solid foundation for your understanding of what it means to become a value-added salesperson.

Specifically, this chapter has the following purposes:

- Define value, value added, and Value-Added Selling
- Describe the characteristics, attitudes, and habits of value-added salespeople
- Share with you inside information on what buyers really want from sellers
- Explain the real impact of discounting on your company
- List the reasons why salespeople fail to sell value-added solutions

What Is Value?

Most people describe value in cost-benefit terms. They weigh the cost of something against its performance. If the performance is greater than the cost, it's a good value. Buyers consider the effort they expend and resources they invest to acquire something. If what they acquire exceeds the effort and resources exchanged for its acquisition, they consider it a great value. According to this definition, the perception of value is subjective. The following formula is a useful way to consider value:

Price + Cost + Impact = Value

Price is acquisition cost, or the price to buy something. *Cost* is the total ownership cost of something. It includes maintenance costs, operating costs, and disposal costs. Some people call this life-cycle cost or total cost. *Impact* is what the product does for the customer. This includes the immediate benefit from using something and the long-range opportunity value of something. What does your product give the buyer the opportunity to do tomorrow that he or she cannot do today?

This definition of value exposes price shoppers as shortsighted. They are. Anyone who considers only the acquisition price deserves whatever misery accompanies that purchase. Acquisition price is only the tip of the iceberg. Smart shoppers know that the real cost of buying and using a product lies beneath the surface. Your job is to educate buyers to help them avoid this mistake; that is, buying because the acquisition price is cheaper.

What Is Your Value Add-itude™?

It's not a typo. How do you define value? From which direction does your definition of value flow: outward from you to the customer, or inward to you from the customer? In other words, are you seller focused or customer focused in your definition?

Value is personal. Like beauty, value is in the eye of the beholder. To some, value is quality. To others, it's service, support, or ease of doing business. There are as many definitions of value as there are people to define it. Value-added sellers define value from the customer's point of view.

Customer-Focused Value

Customer-focused value is viewing what you sell as customers view it—as value received. It's their problem, their need, their money, and a solution with which they must live. The sale should be about the customer. Customer-focused salespeople may say, "Why can't we sell what they want to buy?" Naturally, this sticks as a thorn in the sides of those who want to respond with their own definitions of value: "Why can't they buy what we want to sell?"

Seller-Focused Value

Traditional sellers define value in their own terms. I call this seller-focused value. Some companies with which I've worked have a *field-of-dreams* mentality when it comes to buyers: "If we sell it, they will buy." On the other hand, they say, "If we don't sell it, they don't need it." This is a seller-focused approach to business. It's the old Henry Ford-ism: "You can have any color car you want as long as it's black."

Arrogance surrounds seller-focused value. It's a belief that says, "We sellers know what's best for you, the buyer." Customers avoid this type of seller. They buy from this type of company only when they have limited options.

A fundamental principle of Value-Added Selling is that if you define and sell value in customers' terms, they pay for it with a higher selling price. If you define and sell value in sellers' terms, you pay for it with a bigger discount.

Perceived Value

Perceived value is sensory input. Perception is subjective reality. What I see is reality for me. The only reality that exists in business is in the mind of the buyer. Perceived value is the promise that you make, and it's the sizzle on the steak. It's the qualitative features of what you sell. It's style, brand name, reputation, packaging, and your knowledge. All of these elements have something in common: they make the buyer feel warm and fuzzy about your alternative. Perceived value plays to the buyer's senses: touch, smell, taste, sight, and hearing. It fuels his or her expectations.

Imagine a gift wrapped elegantly in expensive paper. How excited would you be to receive this? The perceived value, created by the gift wrap, builds your expectations. That is the purpose of perceived value—to build higher expectations.

Performance Value

Performance value is quantitative. Performance value is the proof behind the promise of perceived value; it's the steak behind the sizzle. It's the quantitative benefits of what you sell. It's substance over style. It's your profit impact on the customer's business.

Performance value is more objective and easier to measure than perceived value. Buyers can sink their teeth into performance value, for it offers efficiency, performance, productivity, time savings, and other quantitative benefits.

Perceived value fuels buyers' expectations, and performance value drives their satisfaction. You may get the business by creating the *perception* of greater value, but you keep the business through the *performance* of greater value. Both play a role in customer satisfaction.

Customer satisfaction is a ratio: how you perform relative to customer expectations. If you meet their expectations, the result is satisfied customers. If you exceed their expectations, you have delighted customers. If you underperform relative to their expectations, you have dissatisfied customers. You create these expectations with your perceived value; you satisfy them with your performance value.

You can promise anything you want, as long as you deliver on your promises. This value-added sales idiom is a prescription for success: "Promise a lot, and deliver more."

What Is Value Added?

According to the U.S. Department of Commerce, value added is "the difference between raw material input and finished product output." On a practical level, it's everything you do to something from the moment you buy it, sell it, and service it.

A study conducted for the National Association of Manufacturers found that there is 30 percent fat in value added these days. Suppliers are delivering products or services that customers neither want nor need. This happens because sellers have something that the sellers want to sell. They define value in their terms, not the customer's terms. These sellers impose their definitions of value on the customer. When sellers are in love with their own ideas and believe everyone should feel this excitement, they often dictate value to customers. Remember what I said in Chapter 1: It's not value until the customer says it's value.

What Is Value-Added Selling?

Value-Added Selling is a business philosophy. It's proactively looking for ways to enhance, augment, or enlarge your bundled package for the customer. It's promising a lot and delivering more—always seeking ways to create meaningful value and to exceed customer expectations. Look at the key words in this definition: *philosophy*, *proactively*, and *bundled package*.

Value-Added Selling is a philosophy, not just a book, a speaker, a seminar, or this year's company theme. Value-Added Selling must be rooted deeply in your psyche as the way you want to conduct business. It's a maximum-performance philosophy of excellence in all that you do.

As a philosophy, Value-Added Selling is proactive: It's everything you do before price becomes an issue. It's all the value you build in on the front end so that price is less of an issue on the back end. You can't wait for the buyer to raise a price objection and then decide to use some Value-Added Selling on the buyer.

Value-added salespeople sell three things: the product, the company, and themselves. This is the three-dimensional bundle of value to which I refer often in this book.

In the early 1990s, two Fortune 100 companies asked buyers how much value the company's salespeople brought to the table. These companies discovered that their salespeople delivered 35 to 37 percent of the value added that buyers received. How much value do you deliver to your customers?

If you were to leave your company tomorrow and go to work for a quality competitor, how much business would you take with you? I call this the Pied Piper question. If you answer, "Not much," then it's safe to assume that you're not delivering significant value to your customer. In Value-Added Selling, salespeople are a big part of the solution. In traditional selling, they're a big part of the problem.

Your attitude and competence have a significant impact on customer loyalty and retention. Loyalty follows the person. Buyers may prefer a brand, but they reserve loyalty for people—specifically, you! You become the brand for the customer. Increasing your personal value to the customer is the best job security in the world and the most effective way to shield against objections. Your goal is to become so valuable that the customer is embarrassed to give you a price objection.

Value-Added Selling happens when buyers understand the complexity of their needs, feel some motivation to act on these needs, and perceive the value of your total solution. You engineer this sale by penetrating the decision process early, burrowing deep, climbing high in the account, defining value in the customer's terms, and convincing the buyer that your solution exceeds his or her needs.

In Value-Added Selling, your heaviest time investment is on the front end, where you develop an in-depth understanding of the buyer's needs. In traditional selling, the heaviest time investment is on the back end, where you attempt to close the sale. An inverse relationship exists here. The less time you spend on the front end developing your in-depth understanding of the buyer's needs, the more time you must spend on the back end trying to resurrect a dead sale. Your sales time is better spent on the front end, understanding the buyer's needs, wants, and concerns. (See Figure 2.1.)

Value-Added Salespeople

Never presume that the skill to sell is enough. You must possess the will to sell. Success in anything requires the right blend of motivation and

Figure 2.1 Time investment in each stage of the sale

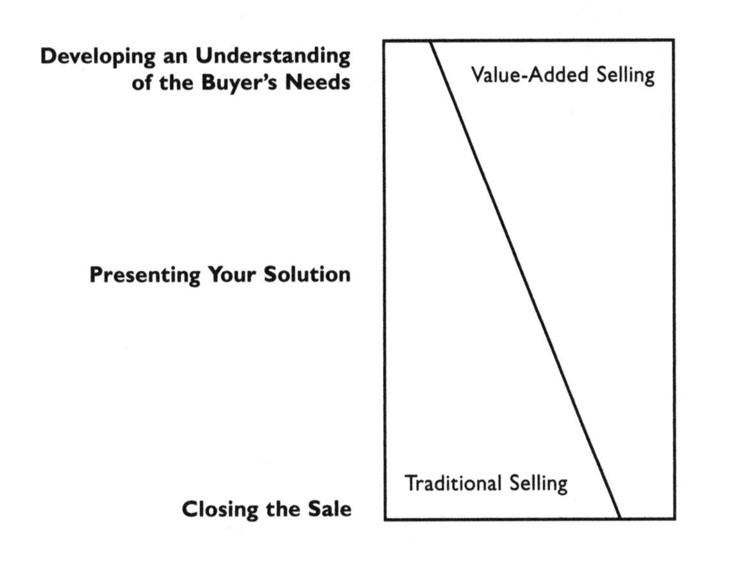

ability—the want-to and the can-do. As someone who has spent most of his educational career studying the principles of psychology, I recognize the importance of observable behavior. But behavior is only part of the story—the visible part.

At the core of motivated behavior are characteristics, qualities, or traits that reflect values. These values shape our attitudes, and our attitudes drive our behavior. Value-added salespeople are people of quality and high character—they inspire trust in other people.

The first chapter introduced you to the concept that organizational excellence is the natural outcome of individual and team excellence. Companies aspiring to become value-added organizations must build them from the bottom up. They establish objectives and marshal their resources to achieve their goals. One of these vital resources is people.

On an individual basis, competency is achieving your objectives. Competencies are the combination of attributes, attitudes, abilities, knowledge, and skills that individuals must possess to perform a job effectively. Linking individual performance to organizational objectives is the purpose of competency-based training. Companies determine what blend of skills and abilities (competencies) are necessary in key job functions that will have a positive outcome on the organization's performance. Then, they hire and train people to achieve these goals.

The following sections read like a how-to list for competency in Value-Added Selling. Comparing yourself against this list of competencies provides a benchmark for self-development. This list describes the value-added salesperson.

Attributes

Years of studying human behavior and working with diverse personalities in sales have given me a unique vantage point to view the characteristics of success that apply to sales. Companies have invested heavily in identifying the magic formula for what works in their industries; in turn, industrial psychologists have responded by generating all forms of psychological tests and instruments to measure sales potential.

Among these tests are behavioral assessment tools, personality dynamic instruments, values inventories, interpersonal measurement devices, and emotional intelligence questionnaires. All boast their unique advantages at providing managers with the insight they desire into someone's personality and ability. Most test developers have a benign motive in designing their tests, and some of these assessments are good at pinpointing what they advocate as success profiles for salespeople and valid predictors of sales success. Nevertheless, having been involved personally in testing salespeople, I argue that testing should be no more than one-third of the decision to hire salespeople!

I have been able to identify three attributes, or fundamental personality dynamics, for long-term success in Value-Added Selling. I call them the Three *E*s: ego strength, empathy, and ego drive.

Ego Strength

Ego strength represents the sense of competence that emanates from a healthy self-esteem. The salesperson has a good sense of who he or she is—strengths, weaknesses, beauty marks, warts and all. Have you ever met someone who resonated self-confidence in an unobtrusive manner—serenely at home in his or her skin? This is high ego strength, versus someone with a big ego. The big-ego syndrome generally results from some insecurity and manifests itself in compensating behavior.

Salespeople with high ego strength draw from a wellspring of healthy feelings about themselves (the essence of self-esteem) and demonstrate positive emotions in these areas: courage, assertiveness, confidence, persistence, creativity, risk taking, and ability to approach strangers.

Value-added salespeople understand that courage is not the absence of fear; it's the management of fear. They feel fear and yet do what they must do: cold call, make tough decisions, and call on customers who intimidate them. Value-added salespeople persist in the face of rejection and persuasively assert their point of view when they believe others must hear their message.

Because of their ego strength, value-added salespeople will explore new possibilities when they approach challenges and problems. This creativity boosts their confidence because they know there is more than one way to skin a cat—they see endless possibilities. This feeds their optimism, which is great spiritual nourishment for salespeople. Because they don't attach self-worth to commercial success (their esteem comes from within), value-added salespeople rebound quickly from disappointment; they are resilient.

Empathy

Empathy is the ability to define life in terms bigger than oneself: "Life is bigger than I am." Humility is nature's way of balancing pride. Value-added salespeople understand that the world spins on its own axis, regardless of their efforts. A strong measure of this attribute bolsters salespeople in getting the focus off of themselves, versus the big-ego type who is always "me-deep" in conversation.

Because they are empathic, value-added salespeople see the customer's point of view. Earlier, I called this the customer value focus. These people view the sale as more than a transaction and the customer as more than an account number.

Empathy is a necessary precursor to being fully perceptive. Effective salespeople use their interpersonal radar to detect subtleties in relationships. The only way to develop this perceptive ability is to open oneself to others. Get the focus off of you.

Empathy is vital to teamwork, and Value-Added Selling is a team sport. To be a team player, you must be willing to subordinate your ego for the greater good of serving others. Whether working with customers, interacting with peers, or coordinating with the boss, value-added salespeople embrace the philosophy that "We is greater than me." High-empathy salespeople play well with others in the sandbox of life.

Ego Drive

Ego drive is the energy to make it all happen. Some people call this motivation; I call it the *want-to*. It goes beyond desire, to include action. Value-added salespeople demonstrate this attribute in their ambition, will to succeed, and initiative. Value-added salespeople make it a habit to do what others consider to be a hassle. They exude a conscientious, can-do attitude.

Their ambition, will to succeed, and initiative are formidable allies when they must summon the energy for challenging goals and determined pursuit.

An interesting blend of ego strength and ego drive girds value-added salespeople with the confidence and horsepower they need in order to feel in control of their environments. They are captains of their ships, masters of their destinies, and architects of their futures.

Attitudes

We move in the direction of our thoughts and feelings; we become what we think about. At the core of motivated behavior lie values. Values shape attitudes and beliefs, and attitude drives behavior; we behave as we believe. Behaviors repeated over time become habits. To fully understand value-added salespeople, you must first understand what they value: integrity, knowledge, equity, excellence, time, service, and teamwork.

Integrity

Value-added salespeople embrace the attitude that trust is the currency of great relationships. When people trust each other, they work out the details. Therefore, they conduct their business in ways that inspire trust in other people and develop the habit of telling the truth. They have discovered that the real benefit of always telling the truth is that you don't need to remember the lies.

Knowledge

Value-added salespeople embrace the attitude in Sir Francis Bacon's quote, "Knowledge is power." For value-added salespeople, Bacon makes sense. They study, read books, attend seminars, listen to tapes, and ask lots of questions. They develop the habit of continuous investment in their personal growth and development.

Equity

Value-added salespeople embrace the attitude that people want to get as good as they give—that business should result in a mutually beneficial outcome. Therefore, they promise a lot, but they always deliver more than they promise. They create win-win relationships with people.

Excellence

Value-added salespeople embrace the attitude that excellence is intrinsically satisfying. They draw pleasure from doing anything well. Because of this positive addiction to excellence, value-added salespeople make it a habit to go the extra mile. For them, there is no traffic jam on the extra mile!

Time

Value-added salespeople embrace the attitude that time is their most precious resource. Therefore, they plan, set priorities, and remain focused on these priorities. They run their territories, as opposed to their territories running them. They develop the habit of being organized, not agonized.

Service

Value-added salespeople embrace the attitude that serving is a pleasure, not a pain. This means that they define value in customer terms, ask questions, listen to customers, and put the spotlight on customer-centric solutions. They develop the habit of making a difference, not just a deal.

Teamwork and Synergy

Among value-added salespeople, the attribute of empathy has paved the way for this attitude of "we is greater than me"—that everyone is responsible for creating satisfied customers. They know at a gut level that none of us is as smart as or as good as all of us. Therefore, they treat other team members with the same respect they would want their best customers to receive. They develop the habit of working with others to build them up instead of breaking them down.

Knowledge

Competency in any job depends on one's knowledge. This is especially true for value-added salespeople. They believe that knowledge is self-empowerment. Consequently, they invest in their personal research and development—the product over which they have the most control. Here is the vast reservoir of knowledge from which they draw:

- The philosophy of value added and the principles of Value-Added Selling
- Company policies, procedures, and infrastructure
- Company value-added services
- Product features, benefits, and application value to customer
- Customer needs, wants, and concerns—past, present, and future
- Competitor strengths and vulnerabilities
- Market and industry trends
- Business systems and structures
- Technology

Skills

Value-added salespeople draw from this wellspring of knowledge to master the skills of their profession. Value-added salespeople must achieve mastery in each of these skill areas:

- Strategic thinking and planning
- Organizing and managing projects
- Recognizing viable sales opportunities
- Initiating contact with people (prospecting)
- Identifying buyer needs and understanding buyer priorities
- Penetrating accounts thoroughly, at all levels, to generate support and build consensus for the solution
- Brainstorming to create a tailored solution to the buyer's needs
- Convincing the buyer of the value of the total solution
- Negotiating details of the contract
- Coordinating internal resources to help the customer achieve the stated objectives
- Providing logistics support and supply-chain monitoring
- Assuring customer satisfaction
- Re-creating value added after the sale
- Resolving problems and providing service
- Reinforcing the value of the solution
- Leveraging the business into greater opportunities

This is what value-added salespeople do: they help buyers make better buying decisions, provide value-added solutions, and follow up to assure customer satisfaction. Focusing on these competencies will help you become a value-added salesperson so that your company becomes a value-added organization. Your organization's success depends on your achievements. As you succeed, it succeeds.

What Buyers Really Want

Buyers want more than a cheap price. My company, Tom Reilly Training, conducted a 10,000-piece survey of industrial buyers and technical users of products. From our research, we've concluded that most of the price objections that salespeople encounter are self-inflicted wounds. Only one out of six shoppers is a *true* price shopper. A true price shopper is someone who considers only price. There's another segment of buyers for whom price is *an* issue but not *the* issue. In fact, a recent study of industrial buyers found that three-fourths of those surveyed would not shop price if they were convinced that value-added services were in place with the supplier.

In our research on price sensitivity, we found that approximately 80 percent of salespeople use price as a competitive weapon. However, when we asked buyers to rate price on a 10-point scale (10 meaning that price is important), they rated it 7.2; salespeople rated price 8.3. Who's making a bigger deal out of the selling price: the buyer or the salesperson? Who's more preoccupied with the selling price: you or your buyer?

Salespeople who expect price resistance generally find it. If you begin the sales call by anticipating a price objection, you unwittingly create one. Asking questions that put the focus on price encourages buyers to shop price. You would be amazed at the number of salespeople who ask a prospect, "Is price important in your decision process?" Who would say no to this question?

We surveyed 1,000 salespeople and their managers to elicit what they felt their customers would tell them is an acceptable price-range differential for a better total solution for their needs. They told us they believed customers would pay an average of 7.8 percent more for a better overall solution. And yet, this same group said they would give away half, 4 percent, of that acceptable differential if the customer asked for a cheaper price. Who do you think is creating much of this price misery? Salespeople, of course!

Our survey of buyers (from all the major industries and regions of the United States) found that buyers would pay 12.2 percent more for better-quality product than they currently use and 8.5 percent more for better service than they currently receive. We gave them a list of thirty-six variables from which to choose, and they told us which ten were most important to them:

Top Ten List

1. Knowledgeable salespeople
2. Product quality
3. Product availability
4. Ease of doing business
5. Technical support

6. Acquisition price
7. Salesperson's ability to get things done
8. Salesperson's follow-up
9. Product performance
10. Support after the sale

How does it make you feel knowing that buyers rank knowledgeable salespeople at the top of the list? Does your knowledge earn you this ranking? Seventy-six percent of the value added that customers receive comes from knowledge-based activities. Your product knowledge, which enables you to prescribe the correct solution for a given application, is real value. Knowledge that directs you to ask the right questions is real value to the customer. Would your buyers pay more to buy from your company because of your knowledge?

Buyers are less concerned with acquisition price. They are more concerned with equity. They want to get as good as they give. Buyers generally turn to price when they perceive an inequity in what they're giving versus what they're getting. Concentrate on delivering more than you promise and more than the buyer expects—you will live with fewer price objections.

Look-alike services and commodity-type products have created many viable buying opportunities for customers. A failure to differentiate one's solution begins inside a seller's company when the marketing department fails to create enough of a gap between its products and services and the competition. Sales is unable to answer the question, "Why should I pay more to do business with your company versus the competition?"

Are You Cutting Your Prices or Are You Cutting Your Throat?

So, you think it makes sense to cut your prices to sell more products? When deciding whether to cut your prices, be sure that you're not cutting your throat. How prudent is it to employ a low-price strategy?

Let's first examine the psychological impact of price-slashing. How do existing customers perceive your price-cutting strategy? They could interpret it as a tacit admission that your prices were too high all along, and you've been gouging them! They may resent it and reject you. Your strategy backfired! It may even create speculation that additional price cuts are imminent.

This speculation causes a wait-and-see attitude in the marketplace, and it goes like this: "Let's wait and see if the prices will go even lower than they are now!" Remember electronic calculators, video recorders, computers, and cell phones? By the same token, the volatility of the stock market has created this wait-and-see attitude on Wall Street. Investors wait in the wings for prices of stocks to drop before they act.

By lowering your prices, you're setting a dangerous precedent. You're telling buyers that lower prices are possible. If they hold out long enough, perhaps they'll get an even better deal. Most automobile buyers embrace this attitude. Who pays full sticker price for a new car? Nobody! The reason is that no one has to. The precedent has been set. Auto price wars began decades ago, leaving plenty of casualties along the way.

Cutting your prices also gives the impression that your company, personnel, and products are not as good as the competition. You're positioning yourself as number two, three, or four. Inadvertently, you're telling the buyer that you're not as creative as the competition, and your only defense is to quote a cheaper price: "Our strongest advantage is our price!" What's the impact of this on employees? Workers start believing that their quality is lower than the competition's quality. They are less motivated to produce high-quality products. You've created a self-fulfilling prophecy that further diminishes your position in the marketplace.

How does cutting price influence you as a salesperson? Your confidence in your company and product begins to wane. How do you think you would fare in a competitive sales situation in which quality is the single criterion? Is it possible that you've psyched yourself out and you feel noncompetitive? If so, the buyer knows it. It's written all over your face.

Does lowering your prices really make sense? How does cutting price affect your motivation as a salesperson? Do you feel as excited about servicing this customer when he or she gets bargain-basement pricing? Have you ever taken a piece of business and regretted it afterward?

Maybe you even resented the customer because you felt that you got the short end of the deal.

Also consider the pragmatic implications of lowering your prices. Your profit margins erode, which generally means there is less money for research and development, bonus programs, quality control, and administrative support. When you begin shaving resources because of reduced profit margins, you weaken your long-term competitiveness. You create a situation in which you will be less competitive in the future. Consequently, you'll need to cut your prices again to stay in the game. How long can that go on before you're out of business?

For years, people have justified cutting their prices with the assertion that they could make it up through increased volume. If you're selling at ninety-seven cents on the dollar, you can't make it up in volume! The one thing your economics professor failed to tell you is that your company may not be able to handle the extra volume needed to compensate for the reduced profit margin. Extra volume could mean hiring more people and purchasing additional equipment to accommodate the volume. More personnel and equipment challenge the already-suffering profit margins. You've created a chain reaction. Lowering prices means you must sell more volume, which means you must invest in greater resources, which means lower margins, which means you must generate greater volume, which means even greater demands for resources, and so on ad infinitum. Or, it could end up somewhere short of infinity: bankruptcy court!

If you're still unconvinced that lowering your prices can have undesirable consequences, consider this: How much more do you need to sell to compensate for the loss in your gross margins? Figure 2.2 presents a hypothetical example.

In scenario A, you're selling at your normal list price. Your gross profit is 50 percent, and you're earning 6 percent net profit. In scenario B, you've cut your selling price by 15 percent to be more competitive. After all, a 15 percent discount when you're earning 50 percent to begin with isn't that much, is it? However, notice that your direct costs in B (how much the products cost you) haven't changed. Only the selling price changes, which reduces your gross profit. Your fixed and variable

Figure 2.2 Impact of discounting on profitability

	A Sell at List	B Discount 15%	C Increased Volume Needed
Sales Volume	$500,000	$425,000	$610,000
Direct Costs	250,000	250,000	360,000
	(50%)	(58.8%)	(59%)
Gross Profit	250,000	175,000	250,000
	(50%)	(41.1%)	(40.9%)
Variable Expense	70,000	70,000	70,000
	(14%)	(16.5%)	(11.5%)
Fixed Expense	150,000	150,000	150,000
	(30%)	(35.2%)	(24.6%)
Net Profit	30,000	–45,000	30,000
	(6%)		(4.8%)

costs of doing business still apply. But look at the bottom line: you're in the hole for $45,000!

Scenario C illustrates the additional sales volume needed just to ensure that your bottom line stays at $30,000. If you compute the ratios, you'll discover that you need to increase your sales volume to $610,000 at a 15 percent discount just to contribute $30,000 to the bottom line. This is a whopping 43 percent increase in sales just to contribute the same amount of money to your company's bottom line. Can you sell this additional volume? Do you want to have to sell this additional volume?

This example demonstrates the impact that discounting has on your profitability. Be aware of this impact. Selling greater volume can be misleading. You must ask yourself two fundamental questions before cutting your prices. The first is, "What is your company's goal: large volume or greater profitability?" The second is, "Do you want every order or every opportunity?" There is some business that you don't want. Define these parameters in advance, and make a prudent business decision.

Before you discount, try this exercise: Make two lists on a piece of paper. Under the heading "Impact on Our Company," list all the implications for your company when you cut the price. Itemize how price-cutting adversely affects your organization. Under the heading "Impact on the Customer," list all the implications for your customer when you cut prices. Focus on the negative consequences to the customer. You should easily come up with a list of at least a dozen ideas. These ideas are the seeds of your responses to the customer's request for a cheaper price. Go through your list of consequences with the customer, and point out the disadvantages of lowering the price.

Fun Facts Regarding Price

Based on my research and experience, I've compiled a list of important facts to consider relative to price. Use this insight to make better decisions:

- In the absence of all other information, brand name is still the best indicator for quality. This is the latest finding in a market research study in which consumers rank different variables. If you sell brand-name items, buyers perceive greater value in your product because of the quality.
- Market leaders can easily charge more than the competition. If your prices are within 10 percent of the industry average, you'll have little trouble maintaining your share of the pie.
- If you charge more, people perceive greater value. Conversely, there is a reverse trend toward lower-priced goods. If your products are too cheap, people don't want them. They assume something must be wrong with them.
- Buyers are more price sensitive about the necessities in life than the niceties. If it's a frill, buyers don't balk. On the other hand, when buying commodities, they're more concerned with price. When was the last time you heard someone complain about the price of a new Mercedes or Rolex?

- Some price shoppers are actually compulsive personalities; getting a bargain is more important to them than the price. This explains partially the popularity of cable shopping and Internet auctions.
- Some people are situational price shoppers. They may be dealing with limited funds for a given project, and this motivates them to shop price. Under different circumstances, these people may not even challenge your price.

I've trained salespeople from companies that are the least expensive in their industry. These salespeople usually ask me, "Tom, how do I sell against greater value? What can I do to compete with a company that offers better service and quality?" Isn't it ironic that they want to know how to compete with you, the value-added salesperson, while you want to know how to sell against price?

You could summarize most of these facts by saying that the greater the perceived value you bring to the sale, the fewer price objections you encounter. Invest your selling time well. Pursue ways to add value versus cutting prices. Here's the fundamental question to ask yourself: "Are you cutting your prices or are you cutting your throat?"

Why Don't Salespeople Sell Value Added?

With this much compelling information, it makes sense to ask why salespeople don't sell value added. The promise of greater profitability, coupled with positioning your solution as the value-added solution, is enticing. So, why don't salespeople stick to their guns and hold the line on their prices? I've heard several reasons:

- ***Fear.*** Some salespeople are afraid of losing the order. Others fear that the buyer may perceive them as greedy if they charge *too much* for their goods and services, though no one can tell me how much is *too much*. Guilt is the other side of this coin. Some salespeople feel guilty charging higher prices than their competition charges, and they fear the buyer's reaction. Guilt is a cheap emotion that exacts a great price on salespeople.

- ***Lack of confidence in what they sell.*** Some salespeople do not believe that their solution is any better than the competition's. They feel unjustified in charging more than the competition. These salespeople need to do some in-depth soul-searching. They should study their product's features and benefits and their company's value-added services. They should also study the competition's vulnerabilities. If you conclude, after studying, that you're no better than the competition, then you could be working for the wrong company.
- ***Lack of skills or knowledge.*** No one has taught these salespeople to sell value added. They need training in the principles of Value-Added Selling. If this is your problem, reading this book should provide immediate relief.
- ***Projection*** *(one of the more common reasons).* If a salesperson is a price shopper in his or her own life, that salesperson will get more price objections than the average salesperson. Why? This salesperson projects his or her feelings onto the buyer by rationalizing, "I shop price. Doesn't everyone?" He or she assumes that price is important to everyone. If one out of six shoppers is a price shopper, one out of six sellers is a price seller. You sell price because you buy price.
- ***Mixed management signals.*** Managers support Value-Added Selling as long as it serves their purposes. If capacity drops for a month or two, management gets nervous and may decide on a short-term, volume-sales mentality: Sell more at a lower price, and make it up in volume. This confuses customers and frustrates salespeople. If you're a manager reading this, you must display the courage of your convictions. You cannot expect your salespeople to hold the line on prices if you change your mind and blow with the wind.

All salespeople know this maxim: "If you expect price to be an issue, it will be." If you begin your sales call expecting to hear a price objection, you will hear one. Unwittingly, unconsciously, or inadvertently, you will create your own monster. You may not always get what you want, but you will generally get what you expect. If you turn on your sales radar and program it to detect sensitivity, it won't take long to elicit that price objection from the buyer.

Value-Added Selling Review and Action Points

1. To sell value added successfully and profitably, you must enlarge your definition of value. Price is what buyers pay; value is what they receive. You must educate buyers that the value of something is more than its price or cost; it includes the impact value of what you sell—what it does for the buyer.
2. If you define value in buyers' terms, they pay for it with a higher selling price. If you define value in sellers' terms, you will pay for it with a bigger discount.
3. Buyers want something more than a cheap price. As a value-added salesperson, you must sell all three dimensions of value: the product, your company, and yourself. The same product from the same company from two different salespeople represents two different solutions.
4. To increase your value as a salesperson, embrace the attitudes of value-added salespeople and become a serious student of our profession. Study to build your knowledge base and gain proficiency in the skill areas and competencies that will differentiate you from all other salespeople.

CHAPTER 3

THE VALUE-ADDED SELLING PROCESS

Many of the problems that salespeople encounter come from a short-term, transaction-oriented sales mentality. This transactional approach means that they go from deal to deal and from order to order. They view customers as a means to an end.

Value-Added Selling is a philosophy *and* a process; it's not just a sales call. It's a process for bringing maximum value to the customer. Because it's a process, you must understand the strategic impact of your actions on the customer. Value-added salespeople are thinkers and planners.

This chapter is about the process of Value-Added Selling—the steps you go through, the strategies you employ, and the parallel sales activities that mirror the buyer's activities.

Specifically, this chapter has three purposes:

- Introduce you to the Value-Added Selling process
- Outline the strategic significance of your activities
- Teach you how to think about selling

What Is the Value-Added Selling Process?

Traditional, seller-focused approaches to selling concentrate on the act of acquiring new business: filling the pipeline, pitching the product, and closing the deal. Most of the strategies and tactics that salespeople learn for this approach center on writing orders.

Because Value-Added Selling is customer focused, its strategies and tactics concentrate on maximizing the value that the salesperson brings to the table. This automatically expands the time horizon beyond the acquisition point, offering you more opportunities to add value with your product, your company, and yourself. Value-added salespeople understand the buyer's needs from the moment these needs exist, up to and including complete need satisfaction. Thus, value-added salespeople have a cradle-to-grave view of the buyer's needs.

Value-Added Selling mirrors the process that buyers follow to make better long-range buying decisions. The Value-Added Selling process begins with the salesperson's developing an in-depth understanding of the buyer's needs, wants, and concerns. This insight into the buyer's priorities helps the salesperson view his or her solution as value received, not just value added. The process continues through the buyer's purchasing, receiving, using, and eventually disposing of the product that the salesperson is attempting to sell.

Another way to think of the Value-Added Selling process is that it parallels every step of the buyer's Critical Buying Path™. The Critical Buying Path™ is the sequence of steps that buyers go through from the moment that a need exists up to and including disposal of the solution that they have not yet purchased.

This expanded view of the sales process means that the salesperson's job is not limited to chasing new business and writing deals. It includes activities such as helping the buyer achieve smooth transitions, assuring customer satisfaction, and maximizing product or service performance during usage and development.

Value-added salespeople define their role in broad terms. They wear many hats. One is business acquisition and development, but it's not the only hat. They specialize in customer satisfaction, logistics support, applications, expediting, disposal, transitions, and training, to name a few.

The way to become a value-added salesperson is to determine the path your buyer follows and seek ways to add value at every step along that path.

Strategic Overview

It's easier to understand the Value-Added Selling process from the buyer's point of view. The following time line describes how buyers think about their needs, define what they want in a solution, arrange to purchase that solution, receive the needed goods, use the goods to achieve maximum performance (economy and productivity), and eventually dispose of them. Value-added salespeople move on parallel tracks with their buyers.

Imagine a process divided into three commonsense phases: presale (planning), transition (acquisition), and postsale (usage). The presale phase is the planning phase. This includes all the activities in which buyers engage to determine their needs and choose the right solution. The transition phase is pretty much what it sounds like: the buyer places an order, prepares to receive your products and services, and receives the goods; he or she acquires a solution. The postsale phase is the usage phase. The buyer uses your solution and transforms it into something that performs best for him or her. (See Figure 3.1.)

The buyer's needs vary depending on the phase of the sale in which the buyer is involved: planning, acquisition, and usage. The salesperson's role changes and evolves depending on where the buyer is. Value-added sales activities parallel and support the buying activities.

During planning, the buyer's greatest need is for information. The salesperson provides information. During acquisition, the buyer's greatest need is for smooth and seamless transitions. The salesperson assures a smooth transition. During usage, the customer's greatest need is for maximum performance and economy. The salesperson reinforces customer satisfaction.

In the presale phase, the salesperson is in the *offensive selling mode*—pursuing new business. During the acquisition and usage phases, the salesperson is in the *defensive selling mode*—protecting existing business. Defensive selling is not part of most sales training, but in Value-Added Selling, it is a critical part of what salespeople do.

Management is to blame for the lack of attention paid to defensive selling. Most compensation plans and sales quotas are based on acquiring

Figure 3.1 The Value-Added Sales Process®

Presale—Planning (Information)	Transition—Acquisition (Smooth Transitions)	Postsale—Usage (Economy & Productivity)
During Planning, the buyer's greatest need is for information. Buyers study their needs, source a solution, and select the best alternative. Their critical activities include needs assessment, setting priorities and objectives, establishing budgets, etc.	During Acquisition, the buyer's greatest need is for smooth, seamless, and painless transitions. Buyers' critical activities include placing orders, receiving goods, redistribution, handling credits and returns, etc.	During Usage, the buyer's greatest need is for maximum performance, productivity, and economy. Buyers' critical activities include usage and disposal.

Offensive Selling Mode—Pursuing New Business		*Defensive Selling Mode—Protecting Existing Business*	
Focusing	**Persuading**	**Supporting**	**After-Marketing**
• Account Selection • Account Penetration • Customer-izing	• Positioning • Differentiating • Presenting	• Process • People	• Tinkering • Value Reinforcement • Leveraging
During this phase of the sales process, you identify viable sales opportunities, qualify these opportunities, penetrate the accounts thoroughly, and develop an in-depth understanding of the customer's needs, wants, and concerns. You use this information to brainstorm a solution.	This is the phase of the sale in which you polish your image, create distance between you and the competition, and convince the customer that your product or service is *the* value-added solution.	During this phase of the sale, you follow up to ensure that the customer experiences smooth transitions to your solution, receives special attention as needed, and builds strong relationship ties.	This is the sale-after-the-sale: the phase when you look for ways to continue to add value, get credit for what you do, and grow your business. You're an advocate for the customer and liaison for your company. You help monitor the customer's inventory and usage.
You're in the diagnostician role.	**You're in the promoter role.**	**You're in the service and logistics support role.**	**You're in the growth mode.**

new business. Few companies emphasize increasing customer satisfaction with existing customers. I discuss this topic in-depth later in this book.

Value-added salespeople employ four major groups of sales strategies. While all of these strategies parallel the buyer's critical activities, the first two groups represent offensive selling, and the last two groups characterize defensive selling. During offensive selling, salespeople pursue new business. During defensive selling, salespeople protect existing business.

Focusing

Focusing, the first group of strategies, comprises identifying viable sales opportunities, penetrating the account thoroughly, and developing an in-depth understanding of the buyer's needs. Analytical and diagnostic skills play an important role here, as the salesperson embarks on fact-finding missions and behind-the-scenes study and research.

Persuading

In the second group of strategies, the salesperson is still in the offensive selling mode in projecting his or her uniqueness, differentiating the solution, and presenting a compelling argument to buy. Promotional skills and persuasiveness contribute to the salesperson's success at this stage of the process.

Supporting

Once the buyer has placed the order and is waiting to receive the goods, the salesperson switches to defensive selling activities. Supporting, this third group of strategies, includes both process support and people support. The salesperson's logistics skills and people skills play an important role at this stage of the Value-Added Selling process.

After-Marketing

After-marketing, the fourth group of strategies, is the sale-after-the-sale. It's defensive selling at its best. This means being recognized by the customer for all of your value added, looking for ways to re-create value for the customer, and increasing your business with existing customers. The salesperson's follow-up, creativity, and initiative are instrumental at this point.

In the course of the Value-Added Selling process, the salesperson evolves from diagnostician to promoter to expediter to customer satisfaction specialist. Your activities parallel your customer's activities. This is customer-oriented selling at its best. Before determining your next step, you must first determine where your customer is in the buying and selling process.

Value-Added Selling Review and Action Points

1. Buyers advance through various steps in planning, acquiring, and using a product or service. This Critical Buying Path™ offers you a model for adding value. Your Value-Added Selling process should parallel your buyer's buying path.
2. Your sales activities are divided into two categories: offensive and defensive selling. Offensive selling is the new business opportunities you pursue, while defensive selling is the existing business you protect. Invest time in both sets of activities—offensive and defensive selling.

CHAPTER 4

IDENTIFY YOUR VALUE ADDED

PASSION SELLS, ENTHUSIASM is contagious, and knowledge is power. To sell your value added, you must first know your value added. Conviction grows from studying your company's total solution. Your enthusiasm for your value-added solution must ignite and excite the buyer. If you can't get excited about what you sell, how can you expect the buyer to get excited? Study until your head hurts and your bones itch.

Most people I train lack the knowledge and the passion to effectively sell their value added. In most cases, no one has taught them how to view their total solution in value-added terms. Consequently, they are one-dimensional salespeople—they sell product features and benefits. When you sell the product only, you open the door to too many competitors, including the Internet.

This chapter is about expanding the depth and breadth of your knowledge base. I want to help you design and deliver compelling reasons for the customer to buy your value-added solution.

Specifically, this chapter has four functions:

- Define and differentiate quantitative and qualitative value added
- Explore the three dimensions of your value added
- Help you identify your value added
- Offer suggestions for how you can communicate this message to your buyers

There Are No Commodities in Value-Added Selling!

When I owned a chemical distributorship, six companies in town sold the same industrial chemicals, with no product differentiation. We all sold the same lot number and label. It was like having six vending machines lined up, and buyers would choose which machine to insert their money into. We couldn't say that our products were superior to the competition's products; all we could offer were application suggestions. We had only the value of our company and ourselves to sell. My roots in Value-Added Selling took hold in that sales environment.

The same product, from the same company, from two different salespeople is two different solutions altogether. If you disagree, consider this common scenario: A salesperson enters a territory and sets it on fire. Everyone loves this salesperson—the customers, the inside people, the salesperson's peers, and even the sales manager. This rep is promoted and becomes a branch manager somewhere else. A new rep follows into the territory and destroys it. It's the same product, the same customer base, the same inside support staff, and maybe the same company car. The only thing that has changed is the salesperson.

If I had a dollar for every salesperson who has said, "What we sell is no different from anyone else," I could buy my own corporate jet. This claim of mediocrity by salespeople is one of the poorest excuses I've heard for being noncompetitive in a market. It tells me that the sales rep has not put much effort into defining differences. The most benign interpretation is that management has failed to provide the sales rep with the right information. In either case, we're going to fix that problem in this chapter.

You sell a three-dimensional solution: a product with all its features and benefits, your company with its depth of resources and value-added services, and all of the value added that you personally commit to delivering.

It's imperative for you to study your value added and develop a strong message to communicate to your customer. Once you've gone through the exercises in this chapter, you'll never again say to yourself or to others, "What we sell is the same as everyone else." You are unique, and so is your three-dimensional solution.

What Is Value Added?

I answered this question for you in Chapter 2. Many people find it a difficult concept to grasp. In simple terms, it's everything you do to something from the moment you buy it, handle it, and resell it. Value added is both quantitative and qualitative.

Quantitative value added is easy to sink your teeth into and to get your arms around. It's visible, tangible, observable, measurable, objective, quantifiable, substantive, and performance based. It stands on its own merits. You can attach a dollar value to it and a profit impact on the customer.

It's what you do to the product and for the customer. It's the steak behind the sizzle and the answer to the question, "Where's the beef?" It includes cost containment, increased market share, greater efficiency, and competitive gain. These are easy benefits to sell to your buyer. Your toll-free phone number, fleet of delivery trucks, customer training programs, extended warranty, replacement parts, and twenty-four-hour maintenance have quantifiable gain for the buyer. These quantitative benefits help to sell your solution.

Qualitative value added is more difficult to get your arms around. Compared with quantitative value added, it's more subjective and intangible—not easily measured. It offers more style than substance, perceived and felt but not quite as scientific. Some people call it soft-dollar value added. It makes the buyer feel good about your product, your company, and you. It's more of who you *are* than what you *do*.

Qualitative value added describes your resources. It includes brick-and-mortar issues such as the number of locations and the facilities available to the buyer; the management philosophy of your company; the goodwill you've created with customers; the product's brand name; your company's reputation; your company's depth of resources; the number of years your company has been in business; the mint on the customer's hotel room pillow; and the warm, moist hand towel in first class on a long flight.

While quantitative value added stands on its own merits, qualitative value added implies a benefit. Qualitative value added produces a warm and fuzzy feeling for buyers. They view qualitative value added as a security blanket or cushion. It enables them to get a good night's sleep. And what's that worth? Customers know it's important, but they may find it difficult to nail down.

How to Determine Your Company's Value Added

Look at all three dimensions of value: your product, your company, and yourself. First, product value added is what your product does—its impact on the customer. Identify your product value added by considering how your product enhances or improves the following for the customer: profitability, operational efficiency, productivity, performance, quality, safety, ease of use, waste reduction, uptime, durability, consistency, reliability, operating costs, warranty, serviceability, convenience, compliance to specifications, and timeliness.

How does your product add value to your customer's product? Does this product synergy increase competitiveness, attractiveness, and end-user acceptance? How do customers perceive your product: as an investment or an expense? The product dimension of your value-added solution is, at best, one-third the value that the customer receives.

The second dimension of value is company value added. Make a list of the value-added extras your company provides. This is your "Value in Purchasing" list—VIP list, for short. (See Figure 4.1.) This list contains both quantitative and qualitative value added. It includes literature, reputation, industry leadership, facilities, technical support, location, systems, depth and breadth of inventory levels, shipping policies, ordering options, ease of doing business, distribution channels, field support, Internet support, electronic commerce, free delivery, hours of operation, customer loyalty programs, disposal, trade-in policy, and so on. When designing this VIP list, go for quantity initially and then fine-tune it.

Figure 4.1 Your company's value added

Value in Purchasing (VIP) List

1. ______________________________
2. ______________________________
3. ______________________________
4. ______________________________
5. ______________________________
6. ______________________________
7. ______________________________
8. ______________________________
9. ______________________________
10. ______________________________
11. ______________________________
12. ______________________________
13. ______________________________
14. ______________________________
15. ______________________________
16. ______________________________
17. ______________________________
18. ______________________________
19. ______________________________
20. ______________________________

Get input from many people. Brainstorm with your peers and your boss. The employees delivering the value added are closer to the value added than you are, and it's on their minds. Others in your company may also be able to articulate this value added for you.

Finally, the third dimension of value is your performance—what you do for the customer. The easiest way for you to arrive at your value added is to refer to the Value-Added Selling process explained in Chapter 3 and determine how you add value at each step along the path. (See Figure 4.2.)

In the planning (information) phase, for instance, you may add value by conducting an in-depth needs analysis, providing a live demonstra-

Figure 4.2 How salespeople add value

Planning Phase	Acquisition Phase	Usage Phase

tion of your product, studying the buyer's needs and brainstorming a solution, locating hard-to-find items for the buyer, and submitting a professional proposal.

In the acquisition (transition) phase, you may add value by assuring smooth, painless, and seamless transitions to your product. Your value-added activities could include confirming order status, expediting, tracking back orders, providing training for employees, following the supply chain, and helping with credits and returns.

In the usage (transformation) phase, you add value by following up to assure maximum performance and economy from your product. This postsale support, coupled with helping customers' businesses grow, will differentiate you from all other salespeople with whom your customers meet. Present this chronology of value added as a flowchart to describe how you will support them from cradle to grave.

How to Use the VIP List

The primary use of your VIP list is to communicate your total value to the buyer. Once you've detailed all three dimensions of value—product value, company value (as in Fig. 4.1), and personal value (as in Fig. 4.2)—combine the information into a master VIP list.

You could turn this compilation into a brochure, a handout on your company letterhead, a website page, a sheet in your proposals, or a collateral literature piece to combat price objections.

One salesperson uses this list as a supplier performance appraisal. Twice a year, he audits his company's performance against the VIP list to ensure that the customer receives all the value on the back end that he promised on the front end.

Another salesperson gives the VIP list to his buyer to use as an internal sales piece to sell others within the buyer's company on the salesperson's value added. He had discovered that his internal champion did a better job of selling for him when armed with a support piece explaining his company's value added.

Managers can use this VIP list as a training tool. One of my clients conducts a VIP exercise every January to ensure that his sales force understands the depth and breadth of his company's value added. He begins with a blank flip chart page, and his salespeople fill that page and several others with examples of their value added during the sales meeting. This is one way to keep his salespeople focused on their total solution. Also, it's a great tool to use with new hires to cut their learning curve for the company's value-added solution and to brace them for handling price resistance.

The only limitation to your using the VIP list is your imagination. There are as many ways to use this list as there are salespeople.

Value-Added Selling Review and Action Points

1. To determine your company's value-added solution, consider all three dimensions of value: product features and benefits, company value-added services, and your personal commitments to the buyer.
2. When presenting your value added, include qualitative and quantitative value added. Compose a Value in Purchasing list to demonstrate to the buyer the total value of your solution.

PART II

VALUE-ADDED SELLING STRATEGIES

IN PART II, I explain the strategic side of Value-Added Selling. Strategy answers the question, "What should I do to sell value added?" Your Value-Added Selling strategy is your master plan to direct your selling efforts. It's the link between your dreams and reality. The methods you use to implement this plan are the eleven Value-Added Selling strategies listed in this part. These eleven strategies fit into four categories:

Focusing. This involves value-added target (VAT) account selection—targeting the right customer; target penetration—penetrating the account thoroughly; and customer-izing—learning how to think as customers think.

Persuading. This involves positioning—shaping an image in the customer's mind; differentiating—expanding the gap between you and the competition; and presenting—offering a compelling argument for why the customer should buy your solution.

Supporting. This involves serving—process support; and relationship building—strengthening bonds with your customers.

After-Marketing. This involves tinkering—looking for ways to re-create value added for the customer; value reinforcement—getting credit for the value added your company delivers; and leveraging—growing your business with existing customers.

Here are some key points about these Value-Added Selling strategies:

- Even though I present these strategies sequentially, many of them occur simultaneously and out of the order from which I present them.
- These strategies involve both face-to-face and behind-the-scenes activities.
- Before determining which Value-Added Selling strategy to use, you must consider where the customer is in the buying process.

Fundamentally, value-added salespeople chase the right business, penetrate accounts thoroughly, think as customers think, position their solution as the value-added solution, distance themselves from the competition, present a compelling reason for the customer to buy, support the customer, build strong relationships with customers, seek ways to create additional value, reinforce their efforts in the customer's mind, and leverage their sales opportunities.

CHAPTER 5

VALUE-ADDED TARGET ACCOUNT SELECTION

Focusing is the first of four major groups of strategies that value-added salespeople employ. For value-added salespeople, focusing means targeting the right business; penetrating the account thoroughly; and developing an in-depth understanding of the buyer's needs, wants, and fears.

One of the great challenges I've faced in sales training is helping salespeople who chase the wrong business. Many of them come to my seminars because they have a marketing problem, not a sales problem. They are pursuing business in segments where they are noncompetitive. Some are suffering from what I call the Mount Everest effect—they chase the business because it's there.

This chapter discusses identifying and pursuing the right business for you and building your future on the right business foundation. This means getting maximum return on your sales time invested and learning how to think and approach your territory strategically.

Specifically, here's what this chapter sets out to do:

- Explain the power of discernment and how it helps you make better decisions about using your sales time
- Present you with some ideas to help you understand your markets better
- Show how you can use this market knowledge to select viable target accounts
- Suggest questions that help you develop an in-depth understanding of your target accounts

The Power of Discernment

Do you want every order, or do you want every opportunity? When I pose this question in seminars, I'm amazed at how quickly some attendees respond with, "Every order." They jump at the chance of getting an order. Others in the group respond more prudently: "I want every opportunity. There's some business I don't want, but I at least want the opportunity to turn it down." This is how value-added salespeople think—strategically.

There is some business that you would like the competition to have: some of that low-margin, high-aggravation-factor, slow-pay, no-pay business! In fact, you want your competitors to get as much of that as they can handle. Yet, you want the opportunity to turn it down.

To paraphrase George Orwell, all customers are equal—some are just a little more equal than others. All customers deserve the courtesy and respect of the value-added attitude, but not everyone wants, needs, or deserves the intensity of the value-added sales effort.

Peter Drucker has written magnificently on managerial effectiveness. In his book *The Effective Executive* he points out that being effective is not just knowing *what* to do; it's also knowing what *not* to do. This is the power of discernment.

We can extrapolate for salespeople and say, "The mark of a good salesperson is knowing which business to pursue. The mark of a great salesperson is knowing which business *not* to pursue." When you develop this power of discernment, you acquire a *sixth business sense* that gives you a nose for good business and bad business.

If you are confused about the type of business your company wants you to pursue, discuss it with your boss. Seek clarity regarding the business the company wants you to go after as well as the business it wants you to avoid.

Developing Market Savvy

What type of business do you want to pursue? What type of business do you want to avoid? What do you know about your industry? How many different segments of the market does your company serve?

Which is the most profitable segment? What is good business for your company, considering its long-range plans? On what type of foundation must you build the business? Where can you have the greatest impact with your solution?

Your collective knowledge about your industry, market, competitors, and customers is your market savvy. Answering the foregoing questions helps you effectively direct your sales efforts.

Our research indicates that most industries have four segments represented by a bell curve. (See Figure 5.1.)

The segment on the left side of the curve is the Value-Added Target segment. These are the innovators in an industry—those willing to take risks and to experiment with new ideas. They embrace advances and are always in the vanguard of change. They perceive value added as a competitive advantage. These buyers are sophisticated, well informed, and involved throughout the life cycle of your product or service. This segment represents about one-sixth of the market.

The segment to the extreme right comprises the price shoppers. These are the true price shoppers discussed in Chapter 2, and you're wasting your time selling value added to them. They rarely pay for value added. This segment also represents one-sixth of the market. If you allow this segment to become more than 50 percent of your business, you have positioned yourself as a discount house.

Another problem with targeting this price-only segment is that once you begin to do business here, you adopt some of these customers' characteristics as you adapt to their thinking. Birds of a feather flock together.

The two-thirds segment in the middle is up for grabs, and these people could go either way. They are undecided as to what is more important to them—price or value added. This segment holds promise for you as a value-added salesperson.

Your immediate focus, then, is the one out of six accounts that is a Value-Added Target (VAT). Your success in Value-Added Selling correlates to your ability to identify and pursue this segment.

Viability criteria will help you. Viability criteria define this VAT segment and answer the question, "What is good business for our company?" Here is a sample list of viability criteria that I use in seminars to help salespeople focus on this VAT segment: innovative thinkers,

Figure 5.1 Target segments

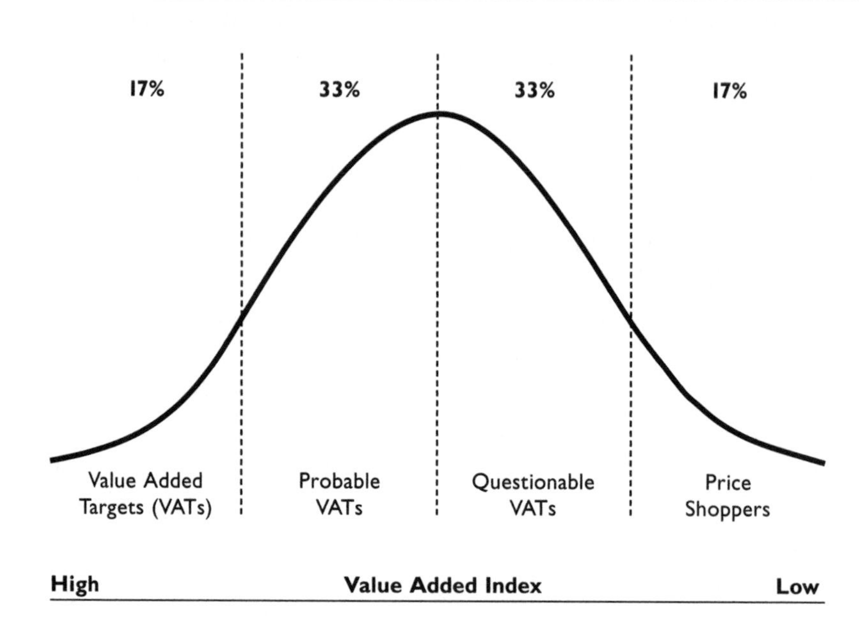

profitability of the sale, longevity of contracts, leveragability of the business, ease of doing business, equitable return on your investment, and cultural consonance. Cultural consonance means that the buyer's company culture looks a lot like your company's culture. This includes the notion that the buyer's company sells value-added solutions to its customers; at a gut level, the buyer understands the importance of value-added solutions.

Notice that this exercise concerns the *type* of customer that is good business, not specific customers. That comes next.

This exercise helps you build your market savvy. What is good business for your company? If you don't know, ask your boss.

Targeting Accounts

Now that you're equipped with an understanding of your market, you can use that information to select specific accounts that fit the VAT profile. Begin by identifying customers who meet your list of viability criteria.

Another way to target VATs is to profile your best customers. First, list your six best accounts. *Best* can mean anything: volume, profit, product mix that you sell to them, or any other consideration you deem important. Next, identify three common denominators of these best accounts. It could be their size, revenue, number of employees, Standard Industrial Classification (SIC) code, location, or a host of other industry-specific variables. The more of these search criteria you can pinpoint, the better the results. With this data in hand, refer to your list of prospects and select six accounts that match the common denominators of your best customers. The acid test for prospecting is that, on paper, your best prospects resemble your best customers.

Once you have selected your six VATs, you're ready to move to the next step in targeting: studying a specific account. The following groups of questions will help you develop an in-depth understanding of this customer's business and identify opportunity areas where you can make a real difference with your solution.

Situation Analysis

- Does this account represent a leader or a follower in its industry?
- Is this account a product-innovative company, a service-oriented business culture, or a low-cost provider?
- Where is this prospect headed (long- and short-term goals)?
- What are the three most important trends affecting this prospect's industry?
- What outside forces are applying pressure to that industry?
- Who are this prospect's customers, and what do they want from your prospect?
- Who are this prospect's competitors?
- What are this prospect's competitive strengths and weaknesses?

Summary of Buyer Needs

- What is this prospect looking for in a product, a supplier, and a salesperson?
- What does this prospect want more of and less of?

- How does this prospect define value?
- What pressure points affect this buyer? (I elaborate on this later in the book.)

Key Player Profile

- What is this prospect's power base distribution?
- Who are the decision makers, and what is their decision process?
- What are their priorities and concerns?
- What motivates these decision makers?
- What are their fears?
- Who are the influencers in this account?

Competitive Information: Describe Your Competition

- How does the prospect meet current needs? (What supplier is the prospect using now?)
- What does the prospect like about this solution?
- What problems does the prospect experience with this solution?
- How do these problems affect the prospect?
- How is your competitor vulnerable in this account?

Opportunity Areas: Dream for Your Customers

- What does this prospect want to be able to do tomorrow that can't be done today?
- What is his or her biggest headache?
- What does the prospect hate to do that we can do instead?
- What are this prospect's profit and resource piranhas?
- What does this prospect need in order to become more competitive in the market?
- What opportunities does this prospect miss but would like to pursue?
- What type of solution would the prospect ideally like to have that no one seems to offer now?
- What would cause this prospect to pay more to do business with us?

Goals

- What are my short-term goals for this account?
- What are my long-term goals for this account?

Strategy

- What is our best solution for this account?
- What can we do to bring more value to this relationship?
- What resources can I use to sell this concept to the prospect?
- What is my selling strategy to achieve these account goals?

When I ask salespeople in my seminars to review these questions for their top customer, most of them tell me they cannot answer all of these questions. This exercise makes them painfully aware that they need to learn more about their customers.

According to national statistics, fewer than one in four salespeople have a detailed plan of attack for their top customer. This amazes me, because your plan is the link between dreams and reality. How can you make a difference for the customer without a plan?

Ask and answer these questions for six of your VATs. If you attempt to perform this analysis for all of your accounts, you won't finish. I'm a realist. You can do it for a handful of your VATs. Once you do, you'll find that the strategic thinking ability that you develop from this activity will also help you with those other accounts: you will automatically process information about other accounts using this questioning format.

VALUE-ADDED SELLING REVIEW AND ACTION POINTS

1. It's important for you to know which business to pursue; it's imperative for you to know which business *not* to pursue. Make a list of the types of accounts that you want to pursue including the viability criteria that define good business for your company.
2. Once you have identified viable opportunities, study these accounts using the questions provided in this chapter, and formulate your strategy based on your research.

CHAPTER 6

TARGET PENETRATION

WHILE TARGETING VALUE-ADDED accounts is one part of focusing, target penetration is another part. Many salespeople enter the decision process late and at the wrong level. They fail to take advantage of a simple Value-Added Selling principle: Few things are as powerful as the right idea, at the right time, in the right place, and for the right person.

This chapter is about timing and buying criteria, generating support for your ideas throughout the buyer's organization, and making sure that you're dealing with people who can say "yes" to your solution.

Specifically, this chapter addresses the following strategies:

- Penetrating the decision process early
- Penetrating the account deep
- Calling at the highest levels in the account

Penetrate the Decision Process Early

The early bird gets the worm. If you enter the decision process early, you have an opportunity to sell the uniqueness of your solution in a way that overshadows the competition. When you enter the decision process late, the buyer places a greater emphasis on price, as you find yourself selling against a competitor's product versus meeting the buyer's needs.

Buyers make purchasing decisions based on their interpretation of their needs, wants, desires, objectives, and constraints. Entering the decision process early means you can help buyers develop a more in-depth understanding of their needs and shape their perceptions of how your solution uniquely addresses their primary concerns. You may have a chance to help write the specifications.

Early penetration in the budgeting phase also gives you the chance to educate buyers so that they have more realistic expectations about what they can get for their money. If they have underestimated their budget, now is the time to help them adjust it. This is an easier task to assess early, versus late, in the decision process.

I was sharing these thoughts one day in a client seminar when the president of the company stood and said to the group, "Ladies and gentlemen, every significant piece of business that we lost this year to price resulted from our entering the decision process too late. We were constantly selling from a defensive posture versus an offensive position. We never had a chance to shape the buyer's criteria in a way that would call attention to our unique strengths."

Entering the decision process early positions you as a team member. You're there from the start, which means the buyer sees you as a partner—someone with an insider's view and an in-depth understanding of his or her situation. As you establish trust early in the process and build a solid relationship with the buyer, you make it more difficult for the competition to gain a foothold in the account. The best defense is a great offense.

Penetrate the Account Deep

Your objective is to penetrate the account thoroughly. Surround the account. Become a professional mole, and burrow your way throughout the account. The more contacts you make within the account, the more supporters you have singing your praises. These are your internal champions.

Every successful sales and marketing campaign has both *push* and *pull* dynamics working in its favor. *Push* is the business you pursue, and *pull* is the business you attract. In sales, pull is the support you generate for your ideas inside the buyer's organization. This support takes the form of internal champions who promote your solution from within the buyer's company.

When I sold industrial chemicals, I viewed this deep account penetration as sales training. In effect, I was training an inner army of salespeople who would sell for me when I was not there. These salespeople would champion my cause. They formed my intelligence unit. I could get inside information from them on the ultimate decision maker and what I needed to do to move the sale along a path favorable to me. I thought of them as my mole patrol.

The most dramatic example I've seen of this concept involves my company and a printing salesman. He did not impress me; I perceived him as too new in his job and too inexperienced for our needs. However, my office staff convinced me that what he lacked in experience he made up for with his initiative.

I remained unconvinced until one of my folks said to me, "Tom, does it really matter if you like him? After all, we're the ones who have to work with him." I deferred to their searing logic, and he did a good job for us. This is a case in which the salesperson's internal champions sold for him better than he did. Who is selling for you while you're reading this book? Who are your internal champions? Do you have a mole patrol?

Penetrate the Account at the Highest Levels

The single greatest Value-Added Selling opportunity area for you today is to call higher in your customer's organization. Few salespeople feel comfortable with high-level calling. This is a significant enough issue that I've dedicated a chapter to Hi-Level Value Added Selling™ in Part IV of this book. I also conduct a separate seminar on this topic.

How high should you penetrate the account? You must call high enough until the person with whom you're meeting can approve the funds for your ideas. Many people in a company can say "no" to an idea, but few can say "yes." A great rule of thumb is to never accept "no" from someone who cannot say "yes." Why would you allow a lower-level decision maker to control your efforts or limit your sales destiny? If the buyer does not have budget authority, you're not calling high enough in the account.

High-level decision makers (HLDMs) have the authority to create money for an idea they like. If you're not calling on an HLDM, you're not calling high enough, period. If you're uneasy with this concept, 90 percent of your peers agree with you. That's how and why they lock in at lower levels. Consider the wonderful opportunity that exists for you since most salespeople do not call on the HLDM. The noise level for calling on the HLDM is incredibly low. Value-added salespeople make it a habit to do what others can't or won't do.

Here's an example. One day, I met with a vice president of sales along with his boss, who was the vice president of marketing, and the president of the company. I was proposing a training solution for five hundred salespeople. My fee splits two ways: time and materials. While no one objected to my fee, the vice president of sales and the vice president of marketing both challenged my materials cost because it exceeded their budget constraints. The president of the company countered, "The heck with the budget. I like the program. Find the money." That's Hi-Level Value-Added Selling™! Had I met with only the two vice presidents, I would have fought a significant price battle. If you're not calling on the HLDM—the one person able to give your price a nod—you're not calling high enough.

Levels I-II-III Decision Makers

The Level I-II-III concept is a simple way to explain the different levels of decision-making authority in a company. Assuming you penetrate the decision process early, you can use this Level I-II-III concept to plan your sales strategy. A decision maker in a given level perceives his or her situation differently from members of the other two levels. Each wants level-appropriate solutions. Your challenge is to frame your ideas within the context and content of the person's level-specific perceptions, needs, wants, and concerns.

Level-I Decision Makers: Logistics Buyers

Level-I decision makers are logistics buyers. They may be purchasing agents, buyers, materials managers, storeroom clerks, office managers, or anyone else involved in the acquisition of products or services. Their common denominator is what they need in a solution. Level-I buyers are primarily concerned with logistics: price, delivery, lead time, packaging, freight issues, credits, returns, payment terms, and so forth.

These lower-level buyers have limited authority, which varies with the organization. Level-I buyers may be able to shift business around depending on supplier relationships, but they rarely have the authority to create money for ideas they like. They process orders that someone else generates. They fill requests; they are responsive by their job description and function. They are the purchasing and procurement arms for most organizations. Their time horizon is short-term and transaction oriented. Did I mention that they are especially price sensitive?

Even though Level-I's have limited authority to buy on their own, you must establish strong relationships with them. They are critical to your success. Level-I's can make your company look bad if they don't like you. Conversely, they can give you the benefit of the doubt when you need it. Can they create pull for your solution? The most underappreciated people in companies are Level-I buyers. They hear from their internal customers only when their internal customers don't have what they need when they need it. Your Level-I's greatest fear is the phone call at 2:00 A.M. with the caller wanting to know where the inventory is.

With integrated supply and outsourcing, Level-I buyers are on the endangered species list these days. They are anxious about their futures. Help them look like heroes, and you have supporters for life. They may *need* logistics support, but they *want* security and genuine appreciation.

Level-II Decision Makers: Influencers

Level-II decision makers are user-influencers. These mid-level decision makers include maintenance people, safety officers, equipment operators, users of the product you sell, technical influencers, resellers of your product (if you sell through distributors), and operations managers. The priority of Level-II influencers is usage: ease of operation, maintenance, efficiency, conformity to specifications, technical support, product performance, safety, and user-friendliness.

Level-II influencers have user-type concerns: quality, function, deployment, and operation. They use the product, operate it, maintain it, supervise others who work with it, must have it as a part of something they create, or resell it to their customers.

Level-II's have influence over the sale because they can specify a product, a brand, or a supplier. They generate requests that the Level-I's process. Level-II's also create pull for your solution. Conversely, their rejection of a product on technical or functional grounds can be the kiss of death for a salesperson. The time horizon of Level-II's is longer than that of the Level-I buyers. Unlike the Level-I buyer, Level-II's think beyond the acquisition point to how the product or service will make their lives better as they use it.

With the Level-II on your side, you have an internal champion to sell for you when you're not there to do the job yourself. The Level-II can be a sounding board for new ideas that you want to present to upper-level management. This person can be your guide through the organizational maze of decision making.

Level-II decision makers may need a quality solution, but they want you to make their lives better, safer, and easier.

Level-III Decision Makers: HLDMs

Level-III decision makers represent upper management. These HLDMs are company executives, high-level managers, business owners, and directors. Level-III's think differently from Level-I's and -II's. Level-III's stress profitability, cash flow, competitive posture, employee issues, customer satisfaction, industry trends, and shareholder value.

Level-III's have the authority to use money any way they see fit to achieve organizational objectives. This is what determines a Level-III buyer, or an HLDM—the authority to create funds for an idea. However, many will defer to a lower-level influencer for input. If a Level-III likes your idea, it's a safe bet that you will get the business. That's why you must penetrate the account at this level.

The time horizon for Level-III's is long-term. They think in years. They think, plan, and execute strategically. Fundamentally, they want to know how your solution fits into their long-range growth plans. Beware. They do not buy products. They form strategic partnerships. In Chapter 23, I cover this topic more thoroughly.

Figure 6.1 tabulates the three-level needs hierarchy.

Figure 6.1 Levels I-II-III needs hierarchy

	Needs	Wants	Fears
Level III	Industry trends Company direction Competitive challenges Outside pressures (government) Missed opportunites Profit piranhas Underutilized resources Better customer service Reduced cycle time Employee issues Lower cost of doing business Increased efficiency & effectiveness Maximum shareholder value	*Business Owners* Control Freedom Practical Simple *Corporate Executives* Mainstream Consensus Career protection Widely accepted solutions Results-oriented solutions	*Business Owners* Loss of control More to do Complexity Having to answer *Corporate Executives* Too much exposure Looking bad Not politically expedient Not fitting in
Level II	Quality standards Service & support issues Creature comforts Productivity issues Maintenance & design issues Training needs Compliance issues Safety concerns Performance standards	Technically proven solutions No guesswork/suprises: CYA Data to make decision Easier to operate/maintain Safe to use Make the job simple Stability/maintain status quo	Suprises No back-ups More to do Unproven ideas Complexity Guesswork Unpredictable variables
Level I	Time Special handling Packaging Lead time Budget Ordering concerns Delivery issues Availability	Appreciaiton Security Respect Safe purchase No ripples	Crises Too much challenge Mistakes Techno-talk No substitutes No loopholes

Value-Added Selling Review and Action Points

1. Penetrate your accounts *early* to help buyers write specs, *deep* to create pull for your ideas, and *high* to generate funding for your solution.
2. You will call on three levels of decision makers to thoroughly penetrate your value-added target accounts. Each level of decision makers has different priorities—needs, wants, and fears. Study their priorities and present your solution as it satisfies the level at which you're calling.

CHAPTER 7

CUSTOMER-IZING

A FUNDAMENTAL PRINCIPLE of Value-Added Selling is that buyers, not sellers, define value. Too many companies encourage their salespeople to create a need for what they sell, versus understanding the buyer's need and then creating a solution. More U.S. sales training dollars are spent on teaching product knowledge than selling skills. Salespeople interpret this training phenomena as a benchmark for how they should spend time with buyers—talking versus listening. This practice translates into firehouse, feature-benefit presentations in which the salesperson dominates the conversation—a monologue, not a dialogue.

Coupled with targeting and target penetration, customer-izing completes the overall focusing strategy that value-added salespeople use. Customer-izing is learning how to think as buyers think—defining value in the customer's terms. It's developing an in-depth understanding of the buyer's needs and the driving forces behind these needs. It's seeing life from the buyer's unique point of view. Customer-izing allows you to perceive your value added as value received, thus applying your customer-value focus.

While you're developing this in-depth understanding, you help buyers understand their needs more thoroughly. Buyers who understand the complexity of their needs are more open to value-added solutions. Designing a customer-oriented solution positions you as a trusted partner and confidant. The buyer perceives you as an important resource. You're vital to the other person's success.

This chapter is about the face-to-face and behind-the-scenes activities in which you engage to acquire this in-depth understanding.

Specifically, you'll gain insight about the following topics:

- Organizational needs and the driving forces behind these needs
- Personal needs, wants, and fears
- Buyer pressure points that take priority over price

Organizational Needs

Buyers have a complex set of needs that include both organizational and individual influences. I like to use the analogy of the iceberg to illustrate this point. (See Figure 7.1.) The tip of the iceberg represents the obvious: the visible needs. The buyer uses these objective buying criteria to evaluate competitive alternatives. The buyer attempts to satisfy this set of needs when making a buying decision.

Figure 7.1 Needs and wants iceberg

Organizational needs include compliance with specifications, quality, delivery, terms, price, product performance, ordering convenience, and other fundamental buying criteria. It's *what* buyers need in a solution; it's their *buying position*. Fully understanding these needs requires careful analysis, as explained here.

- ***First, what are your buyer's total organizational needs for a solution?*** What are the driving forces behind these needs? These driving forces are the *whys* behind the *whats*. Are there departmental matters to consider? Do you know the buyer's goals, objectives, and overall mission?
- ***Second, what is your buyer's decision process?*** This includes the timetable, people involved, and steps buyers must go through. It also includes how buyers will make the decision. Will they maximize or "satisfice" (sacrifice-satisfy-suffice)? If they maximize, they will seek the best possible alternative to solve the problem, regardless of the price. If they satisfice, they will choose the minimally acceptable option because of its price.
- ***Third, how is the power base distributed throughout your buyer's organization?*** In addition to who's involved, you must understand the relative input of the Levels I-II-III decision makers, as discussed in the previous chapter. Will one department have veto power over another? What political considerations are there? Is an internal power battle going on? When one department battles another, you may end up being a casualty of that war. Understand your buyer's battleground. In Chapter 18, "The Needs Analysis Stage," I offer you a tactical approach to discovering these needs during a sales call.
- ***Fourth, what opportunity areas exist?*** These include areas of dissatisfaction as well as areas of desired enhancement—pain or gain—that are sufficient to motivate change. Turn on your personal radar to identify these opportunity areas. They will provide the emotional catalyst for change. People change when the pain is greater than the gain. When buyers are dissatisfied with the status quo, they will change. If there is an area in which customers perceive an opportunity to improve, they will often act on this desire to achieve a gain. Your job is to snoop around to identify these opportunity areas.

- ***Fifth, what are your buyer's critical issues for this purchase?*** What is most vital to the buyer's achieving his or her goals? This area includes mission-critical activities, the success factors vital to the buyer's success. When you identify the absolutes that must happen for buyers to achieve success, you shift the focus from price. Critical issues may include timeliness of delivery or scheduling, absolute quality standards, technical support during transition, and even the ability of your solution to integrate into the buyer's current procedures.

Collectively, these various needs compose your customer's organizational profile. This is the tip of the iceberg. These are highly visible issues that any curious salesperson who is willing to invest the time should discover. The less-visible issues are the individual's needs.

Personal Issues

One of the great opportunity areas in business-to-business selling is the human side of the buying decision. Business-to-business salespeople tend to underestimate the role that emotion plays in the sale. Emotion drives buying decisions. This statement is true even for the most technical sale. People still buy from people.

Human beings are emotional creatures. We make emotional decisions and often use reason to justify them. If humans made purely rational decisions, no one would smoke, eat or drink to excess, or engage in high-risk hobbies. We listen to and respond to our emotions. When the emotional beast screams, we feed it.

Individual involvement in buying decisions is the personal set of needs, wants, desires, and fears that may lie beneath the surface in my iceberg analogy. In other words, this set of issues is not always visible. In fact, some buyers may attempt to hide these personal needs, wants, and fears. These issues represent a personal win for the buyer. They are the subjective and emotional buying motives that drive the sale. On a personal level for the buyer, they answer the question "What's in it for me?" Here we have an important Value-Added Selling principle: *Buy-*

ers prefer to buy what they need from salespeople who understand what they want to achieve and what they want to avoid.

Buyers make emotional decisions based on what they want to achieve and what they want to avoid—gains and pains. Personal gains include the qualities people want more of: control, image, power, security, stability, ego gratification, greed, and other positives.

Pains or fears include what they want less of: risk, more work to do, too much exposure on something, a call at 2:00 A.M. asking where the supplies are, loss of control, damage to their image, being politically vulnerable, making a mistake, and other negatives.

Selling on both levels—organizational needs and personal wants—gives you a powerful advantage. You create solutions that help buyers achieve their organizational objectives while satisfying their personal goals. Customer-izing is studying this complex set of needs, wants, and fears both when you're with the buyer and when you're behind the scenes. Use this information to customize a solution.

Buyer Pressure Points

This is an area that deserves special attention because of its impact on your negotiation with the customer. Buyer pressure points are factors that cause the buyer to look beyond price. The more pressure points that exist in the sale, the less important price is. Pressure points offer you a window into the buyer's nonprice motivation to buy. Your objective is to identify as many of these pressure points as you can, and use them to draw the emphasis away from price.

Here is a rundown of these pressure points:

- Timing and a sense of urgency—the buyer needs it ASAP
- Uniqueness of the problem that the buyer is experiencing
- Brand preference for what you sell
- Supplier preference for your company
- Critical impact of this decision on the buyer's business
- Availability of supply
- Uniqueness of the solution

- Multiple barriers to direct product comparison
- Other customers competing for your time
- A bad experience with your competition
- Few perceived substitutes for your product
- A painless transition to your solution
- Budget availability—the buyer has the money
- Budget deadline—spend it or lose it
- Healthy state of the buyer's business
- Compliance requirements
- Favorable location of your company
- Negative impact of "cheap" on the buyer's image
- Questionable credit status—the buyer has problems

Notice that timing is number one on the list; when buyers are in a hurry to purchase something, price is less compelling. Likewise, in the face of a brand or supplier preference, price is secondary. If there's a limited-supply situation, again, buyers do not shop price. Do you see a pattern here? The more of these pressure points that exist, the stronger your negotiating position. Your understanding and usage of this knowledge is not permission to take advantage of the buyer. What it does do is help you make prudent seller decisions. Why give away the store?

Look for these pressure points on your sales calls. Turn on your sales radar. Send a follow-up letter to buyers after the sales call, recapping some of the relevant pressure points and using them to rebut price objections. Before succumbing to a request for a discount, review how many pressure points the buyer is experiencing. A negotiating principle is at work here: *Whoever feels the most pressure makes the most concessions.* A solid understanding of this dynamic will make you a better negotiator.

One of my clients told me how a new salesperson on his force used the pressure points concept to negotiate a higher selling price for his company's engineered solution. The salesman was working on the biggest sale this company had seen in a while. The customer asked for a 20 percent discount. When the salesman presented the deal to his company, the consensus among the company elders was that the deal was good, even at the 20 percent discount.

The young salesman said, "I don't believe we need to discount. The buyer is feeling too much pressure not to do business with us. Let's use the pressure point concept and see what happens." The group was nervous about losing this order, but the vice president of sales deferred to the salesman's instincts.

The salesman wrote the buyer a letter recapping the pressure points in a positive way and built a presentation around how his company would help the buyer satisfy his needs while relieving the pressure points. The company got the order without cutting the price. The 20 percent amounted to a $180,000 difference! Not bad for a simple concept, is it?

This strategy of demonstrating positively what the buyer could lose by making a price-only decision is powerful. It saves the buyer headaches down the road when the luster of a cheap price wears off and problems with a cheaper alternative arise. How more customer oriented can you be than helping your buyer make better, long-term buying decisions? This is Value-Added Selling at its best—looking out for the customer's welfare while protecting your margins!

VALUE-ADDED SELLING REVIEW AND ACTION POINTS

1. Customer-izing is learning to think as your customers think—viewing your solution as value received, not just value added. Study your value added from the buyer's perspective to sharpen your customer value focus.
2. Completing a profile of the buyer's needs, wants, and fears means that you must study the buyer's organizational needs as well as personal issues.
3. You can improve your negotiating position by looking for buyer pressure points. These conditions shift the accent from price to other relevant buying criteria. The more aware you are of these pressure points, the more effectively you can sell your value added and avoid price objections.

CHAPTER 8

POSITIONING

PERSUASION DEFINES THE second major group of strategies that value-added salespeople use. Persuasion positions your solution as the value-added solution, differentiates you from the competition, and presents a compelling argument for the buyer to choose your solution.

Persuasion often takes a bad rap. People hear the word and think it means manipulation and mind control. Here's a reality check: Persuasion has existed from the time Eve persuaded Adam to take a bite from the apple. It's around us in everyday conversations. Parents persuade children to make the right decisions. Spouses persuade their partners to accept their points of view. Teachers persuade students to learn. Bosses persuade employees to do the job. Doctors persuade patients to accept treatments. Lawyers persuade judges and juries. And salespeople persuade buyers to purchase. Persuasion is part of life.

Persuasion is more than a conversation: it's every way you communicate your message to the receiver of that message. In persuasion, the messenger is an important part of the message. Your credibility and sincerity influence the buyer's receptiveness to your persuasion.

Positioning, the theme of this chapter, is the first of three distinct persuasion strategies in the value-added selling repertoire. Understanding and using this concept means you create expectations in a buyer's mind about your solution. Buyers use these high expectations to judge every other competitor. Your image thus becomes the standard by which the customer measures everyone else.

Specifically, this chapter has the following purposes:

- Establish four key points about positioning
- Explore the image you project
- Offer some ideas on how to communicate this image
- Explain personal positioning strategies

What Is Positioning?

Positioning is forging an image in the buyer's mind. It's carefully shaping how you want others to perceive you. It's framing your message in a way that supports your communication objective. Positioning is a marketing strategy that salespeople tactically execute to persuade others that their solution is *the* value-added solution.

Here are key points you should know about positioning:

- It's a campaign, not an event. This ongoing process completely surrounds the customer with the message that the sender wants to communicate. This is a well-planned and coordinated effort.
- Positioning happens face to face and behind the scenes. For example, sending the buyer an article about your company is part of your image-building campaign. How you conduct your sales call communicates something about your professionalism.
- Every company owns a position in the customer's mind. What comes to mind when someone mentions your company's name? Do others perceive you as the value-added supplier, or does your solution look like everyone else's?
- Everything you do affects this perceived position, one way or the other. Your company can spend millions of dollars to promote an image, but the way you present yourself and your solution speaks volumes to the buyer.

How Do Buyers Perceive Your Solution?

Value-Added Selling grows from a simple principle: People buy more than a product. They buy all three dimensions of value—the product, the company, and the people. Collectively, this is your solution. What image do you want to project in each of these three areas?

- Product—quality, durability, state-of-the-art technical superiority, and user-friendliness
- Company—ease of doing business, support, commitment to innovation, management flexibility, and stability
- People—helpful, concerned, informed, and customer oriented

To position your solution effectively, you must have a clear understanding of the image you want to communicate. Then you must use marketing to deliver your message. Marketing is every way you communicate with your buyer.

You can use a variety of means to help communicate your position effectively. Send favorable articles to the buyer about your company or your products. Tell the buyer about awards your company wins; some companies make copies of these awards for their salespeople to use on sales calls. Dedicate sections of your customer newsletter to promote your image. Use advertising to shape this image. Infuse your sales vocabulary with terminology that supports your position of value (for example, "One of our value-added services is . . ."). Highlight sections in your literature that reflect the image you want to project. Leave a message on your voice mail that reminds the customer that you are the value-added supplier. Your strategy is to surround the buyer with your message or position.

Personal Positioning

Personal positioning refers to how the buyer perceives you as a salesperson. Others perceive what you choose to project. Every salesperson projects an image to the buyer. Does the buyer perceive you as a deal guy who is interested only in the transaction or as someone who is interested in making a difference? Does the buyer view you as an expert in your field? Are you a valuable resource on whom the buyer can rely? Buyers perceive you as either part of the solution or part of the problem.

Buyers have an imaginary collage of faces on their office walls. In this collage are the faces of all the salespeople they know. Either your face stands out in three-dimensional fashion because you've positioned yourself as the value-added salesperson, or you blend in with the rest of the crowd. Standing out in three-dimensional fashion is a great opportunity area. Your behavior will differentiate you from the rest of the pack.

These factors affect your personal position with the buyer:

- ***Knowledge.*** Most value added is knowledge based. Your knowledge can position you as an expert—an important part of the team. One buyer told me that he depends on salespeople for the majority of the industry knowledge he gathers. Do your buyers perceive you as a viable source of information?
- ***Appearance.*** Do you look like a success? Value-added salespeople dress to the top of their market. Do you dress for success? Perceived value includes personal packaging in addition to product packaging.
- ***Use of time.*** Buyers value their time. They also watch how others use time. Successful people use time effectively. Your efficient use of time communicates the image that you respect this valuable resource. Others will respect your time if you respect it.
- ***Personal organization.*** Do you have it together? Are you organized or agonized? When you make the time to organize your presentation, it shows. When you fail to make the time to organize, it also shows. If you can't keep yourself together, why should buyers think you could pull it together for them?
- ***Effectiveness of communications.*** How well do you communicate your thoughts? Do they make sense to the buyer? Are you easy to follow, or do you ramble incessantly about subjects that bore your buyer?
- ***Quality of presentations.*** Are your sales presentations impressive? Are they convincing? Do you present a compelling reason for the buyer to choose your alternative? How much time do you invest in planning for the sales presentation?

- ***Passion.*** Aristotle recognized that passion sells and enthusiasm is contagious. If you're not excited about what you offer, how can you expect the buyer to get excited?
- ***Sincerity.*** Buyers want to trust sellers. Sincerity builds this trust. The fundamental question that your buyer asks is "Can I trust you?"
- ***Successfulness.*** Do you have a record of success? Nothing sells like success. Buyers like to do business with others who know how to create success. Brag positively. Selective name-dropping works well.

Use this information to polish your image with the buyer. You are an important part of the solution. You are real value. Communicate this to your buyer.

Value-Added Selling Review and Action Points

1. Persuasion embraces every way you communicate with your buyer—it's a process, not an event. What do you communicate to your buyer about your company's value-added solution? What image does your company own in the buyer's mind?
2. Effective positioning is surrounding the buyer with your image of value. How will you continue to support this image and surround the buyer with it?
3. Buyers perceive what you choose to project. When the buyer thinks of you as a salesperson, what image comes to mind? How can you continue to position yourself as the value-added salesperson?

CHAPTER 9

DIFFERENTIATING

More than half of the people I train cannot tell me how or why their solution is better than the competition's. Here's where differentiating comes into play.

Like positioning, the first persuasion strategy that value-added salespeople use, differentiating makes it easier for the buyer to choose your solution over the competitor's. Buyers are inundated daily with hundreds of marketing exposures: billboards, radio and TV ads, print media ads, direct-mail pieces, E-mail advertising, and phone solicitations. Differentiating makes you jump out from the crowd. It's distancing yourself from the competition—expanding the gap between you and the alternatives.

Specifically, here's what you'll learn in this chapter:

- How to identify what makes your solution different
- Suggestions for creating barriers that defy direct comparisons
- Ways to sell your differentiated solution

Your Definable and Defendable Differences

What are your definable and defendable differences? How do you respond to a buyer who asks, "Aren't you and so-and-so in the same business?"

Would you answer, "We're in the same industry, but we're certainly not in the same business, and here's why . . ."? Most salespeople struggle to answer this legitimate question. And I have a theory for why that is.

People spend much of their lives seeking ways to fit in. Everyone needs to belong somewhere. This need to belong is so powerful that people often lose their ability and desire to pursue their God-given right to be different. Little children want to dress as their parents dress; older children want to dress like their peers. Fitting in is an important part of the socialization process. In business, buyers want sellers to comply with specs but justify their differences. Being different is OK on a personal level—God made you that way. In business, it's a survival strategy.

Imagine you're in one of my seminars with fifty of your peers, and I invite you on stage with me. I tell you that you have fifteen minutes to discuss the primary differences between you and your two largest competitors. You blush, your heart rate increases, and you feel a knot in your gut. This is the reaction most salespeople demonstrate when I ask them to join me in front of the group, but I don't let them suffer too long. I tell them that I'm only kidding. They're relieved because they don't know how to articulate the differences.

The best way to determine the most significant differences between you and the competition is to think in terms of the three dimensions of value: product, company, and people. The differentiation matrix in Figure 9.1 illustrates a spreadsheet comparison of three competitors, using thirty-six variables. I use this matrix in my seminars to lead a discussion of competitive differences.

This is a generic matrix, and you can use it for many industries. You may want to tailor this form to your company and your competitors. Add value to the exercise by including some industry-specific variables.

Having reviewed this matrix, how would you answer the question that I led with: What are the definable and defendable differences between you and the competition? Most salespeople respond by saying they need some time to work on it.

Go ahead and study the differences. Seek input and information from other people. Share your competitive knowledge. Be prepared for the buyer's inevitable question: "Why should I buy from your company versus another?" If you can't answer it in training, you won't be able to answer it on the streets.

Figure 9.1 Differentiation matrix

Product Attributes	Our Company	Competitor A	Competitor B
Availability			
Packaging			
Warranty			
Acquisition price			
Quality			
Usage cost			
Durability			
Performance			
Brand-name value			
Efficiency			
Safety			
User-friendliness			
Company Attributes			
Ease of doing business			
Reputation			
Technical support			
Terms			
Return policy			
Inventory levels			
Service policy			
Ordering options			
Management flexibility			
Industry leadership			
Postsale support			
Presale assistance			
Salesperson Attributes			
Knowledge			
Follow-through			
Understanding of needs			
Empathy			
Accessibility			
Integrity			
Straightforwardness			
Innovation			
Listening skills			
Eagerness			
Organization			
Ability to get things done			

Create Barriers

Creating barriers between you and the competition makes it difficult for the buyer to simplify the decision process and choose a supplier based solely on price. Barriers defy direct comparisons. The best way to create barriers and to distance your solution from the competition is to think in terms of what the buyer needs versus what the competition is selling. Differentiate your solution by projecting yourself into the buyer's situation.

Earlier, I argued that value-added peak competitors sell to the customer's needs, not against the competition's package. Putting the emphasis on the customer instead of the competition automatically differentiates you from the rest of the pack. Your competitors devote more attention to their competition's product than to the buyer's needs.

- ***Create barriers by using a time line to present your solution.*** Lay out your solution along a time line that begins with the buyer's need surfacing and ends with need satisfaction. This format gives you a model to present your chronology of value. In doing so, you stretch the buyer's time horizon, calling attention to your down-line value. Stretching the time line moves the focal point away from acquisition prices and onto your long-range solution.
- ***Create barriers by making it easier for buyers to do business with your company than with a competitor.*** This idea surfaces often and in many ways in buyer surveys. Make it easy to place orders, get technical support, and reach customer service. Customers want to do business with companies that demonstrate they want to do business with buyers. Flexibility wins a lot of business for companies.
- ***Create barriers by providing direct access to people who can make things happen.*** Technology has allowed companies to avoid direct personal contact with customers. Elaborate phone systems that promise increased efficiency via submenus epitomize technology's impersonal touch. Buyers say that they hate these systems. If it takes buyers five submenus to get to a real person, they become irritated and agitated. Don't you, too?

How does it feel to run through a series of submenus to get to *hold*? Because buyers get frustrated with these automated phone systems, they pursue suppliers who give personalized attention. Wouldn't you?

Technology is great. I've dedicated a chapter to it in Part IV. However, when technology presents a barrier to customer satisfaction, you must consider an alternative: simply, get rid of the automated phone-answering systems. Your customers will thank you—in person and with sincerity.

Recently, a sales rep told me about a new account he got because the competition put the buyer on hold for an average of twenty-two minutes every time he called. The buyer got mad and decided he would get even by transferring his business to a competitor who did not put him on hold for twenty-two minutes. This buyer managed one of the largest fleets of heavy equipment in the country. Imagine losing business because your company puts a large account on hold too long. Consider the irony of losing business as a result of employing the technology that promises to help you deliver better service.

- ***Create barriers by packaging your products and services in a unique bundle and choosing a different pricing model.*** I'm amazed at the number of suppliers who package and price their goods and services exactly the same as everyone else in the industry. They make it painless for buyers to choose the cheapest alternative. Creating a unique packaging barrier makes it difficult for the buyer to choose solely on price. Why set yourself up for commodity comparisons? It's not just OK to be different—it's advantageous to be different. That's the essence of differentiation. If the buyer complains, explain that the uniqueness of your packaging is only the tip of the iceberg: you're unique in many ways. Why would the buyer pay more to buy from you if you look just like the competition?
- ***Create barriers by offering options at different price levels.*** The subtle message you're sending is that if price is a major consideration, the buyer must look at a different package. Printers are notorious for this. I can't remember ever buying a printing job when the print salesperson submitted a quote with just one price. Printers always demonstrate the cost-effectiveness of buying in larger quantities. They upsell.

Buyers who will eventually need and use the higher quantity can take advantage of the cheaper, higher-quantity prices. This higher-quantity pricing strategy also preempts price objections. It signals buyers that they can get overall cheaper prices by increasing the size of their initial order.

- ***Create barriers by using your creativity—there's no commodity in creativity.*** When you view the buyer's needs, wants, and fears from his or her point of view, it gives you a unique vantage point that will stir your creativity. Think outside of the box when designing your solution. Look for unconventional solutions. That's the essence of differentiation—doing things uniquely.

Ask "What if" questions to direct your efforts: "What if we could do this for the customer?" "What if we could change this?" "What if we could improve this feature?" Stretch to the edge of your imagination. Buyers will pay for creative and fresh approaches to old problems.

Tips for Selling Your Differences

You understand the uniqueness of your buyer's needs and the differences between your solution and the rest of the pack. Now you're ready to stand out from the crowd. How do you sell these differences?

- ***Keep it positive.*** Always take the high ground. Avoid negative selling—bad-mouthing the competition. It's possible, and even desirable, to discuss your unique advantages that happen to be weaknesses for the competition. Put the spotlight on what you do well versus what the competition fails to do. Smart buyers know what you're doing and respect the fact that you are not taking an easy shot at a weak opponent. This is especially important when the buyer has purchased from this weak competitor in the past. He or she may feel the need to defend a previous buying decision or take pity on the underdog. Either way, you lose.

  If the buyer attempts to draw you into a direct comparison, remain focused on your strengths: "We're in the same industry, but we're definitely not in the same business. I'd like to discuss what makes our company special and unique in the way we solve your problems." Resist being baited. Maintain the high ground. You'll feel better about your approach and gain the buyer's respect in the process.

- ***Use comparison tools that spotlight these differences.*** A product comparison matrix offers you a format to highlight your advantages. It's similar to the differentiation matrix in Figure 9.1. In the left column, list the primary comparison variables. Across the top row, list three or four competitors. In each cell of the matrix, place a symbol to indicate which supplier offers a specific product feature. In addition, you may be able to rank each supplier. Did I mention that the comparison variables favor your solution?

  Another comparison tool is a spreadsheet financial analysis that compares your solution with the competition's. You may include acquisition price, energy costs, operating costs, maintenance costs, disposal costs, residual value, and other life-cycle costs. This is a financial justification of your product over its lifetime vis-à-vis alternatives. Later in the book, I refer to this as the economic value analysis.
- ***Get others to sell for you.*** Use testimonial letters to call attention to your advantages over the competition. Encourage buyers to talk to your existing customers who have used other suppliers in the past. Use quotes from third-party endorsers of your product or company. If an outside testing service rates your product favorably, use its analysis. If *Consumer Reports* gives your product a favorable rating, use it to build credibility with the buyer.

  A salesperson I met cited an example of using an outside resource to combat a price objection. He discovered a newspaper article about one of his competitors and its struggle to remain in business because of cash flow difficulties. He saved the article in his wallet. A few months later, one of his customers asked how this same competitor could lowball on a bid. The salesman opened his wallet and gave the buyer the article to read. The customer responded, "I can't afford to deal with them. If they're this desperate to raise cash, how do I know they stock all the inventory I need?"

Is this negative selling? No! The buyer asked, and the salesperson answered. A salesperson should not be reluctant to share such information with the buyer. How could you permit one of your good customers to make a terrible buying decision when you had the opportunity to intercede and save the customer the headaches that result from bad decisions?

- ***Acknowledge the generic similarities between you and the competitor.*** Use acknowledged similarities as a springboard to launch into your value-added presentation. You might say, "Granted, there are some fundamental similarities between the competition and us, but I would really like to focus on the value added that makes us different." At this point, detail your value added that is, coincidentally, a weak spot for the competition.
- ***Create barriers with a "Ten Things to Consider" list.*** Select ten of your value-added extras. List them as statements on a page, and label the list "Ten Things to Consider Before Purchasing." You are calling attention to your value added and encouraging the buyer to use these points as decision criteria. You may also design this list in question format: "Ten Questions to Ask Yourself Before Buying." Your value-added extras are now questions for the buyer to ask and answer before making the buying decision. Asked and answered, your questions should favor your solution.

  I know another salesperson who salvaged a large chunk of business by using this idea. He listed six key differences between his solution and a cheap competitor's offer. He labeled it "Six Questions to Ask Yourself Before Purchasing Lift Trucks." At the eleventh hour, he faxed it to the customer, and he got the order—at the higher price.

Value-Added Selling Review and Action Points

1. Consolidation, mergers, and acquisitions have presented buyers with a confusing array of look-alike products and services. Compounding this problem is that most salespeople fail to differentiate their solution from the competition. To make it easier for the buyer to choose your alternative, you must be

able to answer this question: "What are the definable and defendable differences between you and the competition?"

2. Create barriers that defy direct comparison between you and the competition. You can differentiate along a time line of pre- and postsale value in addition to the three dimensions of value: product, company, and salesperson.
3. When presenting your unique selling proposition, maintain the high ground. It's tempting, even momentarily, to disparage the competition. When selling the differences, point out how your solution is unique, which is generally the competition's weaknesses. The buyer will respect your approach.

CHAPTER 10

PRESENTING

For buyers to pay premium prices for a solution, you must present a compelling argument that explains why your solution is worth more to them than their money. They want to feel that your solution is special. Here's where presenting comes in.

Presenting is, along with positioning and differentiating, another persuasion strategy essential to Value-Added Selling. Presenting is face-to-face communication with the buyer. It's the content and context of your message—substance and style. Your effectiveness in organizing, customizing, and delivering this message influences the buyer's willingness to choose your alternative.

Our model for presenting meets three criteria for value: your message must reflect the buyer's personal definition of value, you must take advantage of your perceived value, and you must demonstrate the performance value of your solution.

Specifically, this chapter features three lessons:

- How to personalize your message
- How to communicate your perceived value
- How to demonstrate your substance

Personalize Your Message

Does your message reflect the buyer's definition of value? Are you acting from a customer value base? Buyers want to feel that you understand their definition of value and have designed a solution that reflects their priorities. This is customer-oriented selling at its best. Consider this: It's their problem, it's their money, and it's a solution with which they must live. Your solution should reflect their definition of value. As you review the following suggestions, remember: a fundamental Value-Added Selling principle is that the sale is more about the customer than the seller.

- ***Use analogies.*** The analogy is a powerful presentation tool because adults act on precedent. They process information quickly and effectively when new messages reflect what they already know. By using an analogy, you ask buyers to make decisions similar to ones they have already made. Their new decisions are consistent with what they've done in the past.

  For example, if you sell office interior furnishings, be aware of the image that the buyer's company promotes in its advertising. The inside of this company's office should reflect the image it promotes in the market. This image is all the more important when the company's customers visit its offices. You're selling continuity and consistency, so the analogy makes it easy for the buyer to understand the benefits of your solution.

  You're asking the buyer to use the same logic when deciding about your solution. For example, you say to your buyer, "You've invested heavily in creating and promoting a special image for your company in all areas of your marketing. Doesn't it make sense to invest in office furnishings that support the image you've created in your advertising?"

  Look for some other area in the company in which the buyer has made a buying decision similar to what you're proposing. Use that previous behavior as justification for the buyer's acting on your suggestion. It greases the skids for moving forward with your idea.
- ***Use buyer buzzwords of value.*** Every buyer to whom I have ever sold had a unique way to describe what he or she wanted in a solution. Listen carefully to the exact wording your buyer uses, and

incorporate this wording in your presentation. Infuse your sales vocabulary with the buyer's terminology. This approach reduces the psychological distance between you and the buyer because you're speaking the same language.

For example, your buyer may use words such as *revenue growth* versus *increased sales*, *productivity* versus *performance*, and *contribution dollars* versus *profitability*. Mirroring specific buzzwords sends a message that you have listened and understood priorities, and you have a solution that sounds a lot like what the buyer wants. Speak your buyer's language.

- ***Sell to the buyer's total needs.*** In Chapter 6, I outlined the different levels of buyer needs: Levels I-II-III. The reality of selling to companies is that more than one department may be involved in the decision process. Cover yourself on all bases. Sell to the logistics buyers, the users and influencers, and the high-level decision makers. Present your solution in a way that all departments can see the potential benefit of working with you: your total solution (the three dimensions of value) meets their total needs.

  Your ability to move from one level to another and from one department to another affects your long-range success. You must develop this flexibility in order to reach your full potential in sales. The versatility of value-added salespeople is one of their great strengths.
- ***Customize, customize, customize.*** Study your buyer's promotional literature, and visit the company's website. Identify common themes, and then fill your presentation with these messages. Following your buyer's communications path is a strong message of parallel thinking. It says that your company operates much the same way as the buyer's company. Companies with similar philosophies should do business with each other, shouldn't they? Birds of a feather flock together. How can the buyer reject your offer when it mirrors his or her thinking and promotional themes? To charge value-added prices or fees, you must customize. Buyers will not pay higher prices for generic solutions.

Maximize Your Perceived Value

Is it sexy? Does it sizzle? Does it have flash? These are questions to ask yourself about how your stuff looks—your style. Perceived value is the *context* of your message. It influences the buyer's expectations. It gives buyers a warm and fuzzy feeling about your solution. In order to generate this feeling, every steak must sizzle. Maximizing your perceived value is a quick way to make a positive impact on your presentation. Perceived value is how something looks, feels, and sounds to the buyer. Does it pop? Does it have splash? Does it make the buyer's blood race?

- ***Dress it up.*** Put your best foot forward. How do your materials look? Do they have instant visual impact? How well do you use color and graphics to communicate your message? The quality of what you present to buyers must parallel the quality of your product. Some buyers are visual processors. Technology and color printers make it possible for any salesperson to add sizzle to presentation materials and proposals.

  If you present a message that your company is the value-added supplier, your materials must reflect that image. If they fail to mirror that image, you create cognitive dissonance; as a result, the buyer rejects your offer because it doesn't feel right.

  Whether it's fair or not, buyers judge books by their covers. I know. I've written nine books, and I fully understand the importance of cover design. If the buyer likes the cover, the book sells. If the buyer doesn't like the cover, the book sits on the shelf. I had to redesign the cover of my first book because the book buyers wouldn't evaluate the product until the packaging changed. We changed it and sold 80,000 copies! Same book. Different cover. Fair or not, buyers judge books by their covers. How is your cover?

  I use a dark blue, gold-embossed, leatherlike cover for proposals. Many times, clients who invest from $50,000 to $100,000 with my company spend the first few minutes of a meeting commenting on how nice my proposal looks. The cover predisposes them to expect a high-quality solution. How is your cover? *Remember, every steak must sizzle!*

- ***Use the value-added sales jargon.*** When buyers hear something often enough, they start to believe it. Form an association between your company's name and the words *value added.* Use these words in your presentations, casual conversations, and correspondence.

  Discuss your value-added services, describe your value-added benefits, and make a list of your value-added extras. Surround the customer with your value added. Make it a word-association exercise. What two words should pop into the buyer's mind when they hear your company name? *Value added*, of course.
- ***Choose positive focus words.*** There are many ways to frame a sales message. Some are positive, and some are negative. Choose positive expressions. Do your buyers want more uptime or less downtime? Do they want greater compliance with specs or fewer rejects? Quicker availability or less waiting time for the product?

  You always have a choice in how you express your message. I know a salesman who lost an order because of the way he framed a benefit. He told the buyer that his product ran so quietly that it was "almost dangerous." The buyer perceived this as a disadvantage and purchased another alternative. From these words, the buyer could think only of the likelihood of an industrial accident. How would you like to lose an order to a benefit—especially one that is supposed to be a differentiating factor?
- ***Present your price.*** There is only one way to present your price. Use the three magic words "the price is." Anything other than that creates doubt in the buyer's mind. "Your price" sounds as if everyone gets a different deal. "List price" signals that there are many pricing levels. Look the buyer in the eye and say, "The price is . . . ." The time to exude complete confidence is when you're asking people for money. A buyer who perceives any wavering or lack of confidence on your part will not purchase.

  For a more complete discussion of this topic, I suggest you pick up a copy of my book *Crush Price Objections* (Motivation Press, 1999). It contains a section on avoiding price resistance, and presenting price correctly is a big part of that.
- ***Present long-term solutions.*** Price shoppers are short-term thinkers, whereas buyers who are involved throughout the life cycle of a prod-

uct relegate acquisition price to one of several decision variables. Value-added buyers think, plan, and purchase long term. Stretch your buyer's time horizon by presenting your solution along a time line that extends well beyond acquisition. Most of the value added that companies deliver occurs during ownership and usage. Unless your buyer is thinking long term, he or she will not perceive your value added.

Present your chronology of value to the buyer by saying, "We support you from cradle to grave, and here's how it happens." At this point, lay out your solution procedurally to emphasize the long-term benefits you offer. Many buyers find it easier to visualize your total solution as you lay it out sequentially and over the long term.

- ***Dress up your proposals.*** Creating proposals is an area in which most salespeople tell me they can improve immediately. Begin with a summary of the buyer's needs to spotlight all the reasons why he or she is pursuing a value-added solution. Include a summary of your value added—your VIP list, as explained in Chapter 4. Offer proof and data to reassure the buyer. Stress that you guarantee complete satisfaction. Insert your Customer's Bill of Rights (a list of those things that your customers have a right to expect from your company: prompt delivery, friendly service, quality products, etc.). Top it off with a personal commitment letter from you to the buyer detailing the personal value added that you as a salesperson will deliver. (You'll find sample letters in Chapter 25.) More value added!
- ***Deliver your proposals in person.*** I understand that days get chaotic, and you're busy. It's tempting to fax your proposal to the customer. After all, the customer has told you to do it. Consider this: Your proposal looks only as good as the fax machine that prints it. If it's one of those older, thermal-paper models, your buyer may need thumbtacks to hold the corners down. And if there is a gouge in the print cylinder, this fax will have a dark scar running top to bottom. Is this your best effort? *Every steak must sizzle!*

  For out-of-town customers, send your proposal by overnight courier to emphasize its importance to you. For in-town customers where logistics prevent you from delivering your proposal in person, use a messenger service. Buyers appreciate the special attention, and it says that you go the extra mile.

Demonstrate Performance Value

Performance value answers the question "Where's the beef?" Performance value is the profit impact you have on the customer's business. It's the steak behind the sizzle, and the quantitative behind the qualitative. While perceived value defines your style, performance value demonstrates your substance. This is the content of your message. Use the suggestions in this section to establish your performance value.

- ***Demonstrate your opportunity value.*** What do you give the buyer the opportunity to do tomorrow that he or she cannot do today? This is the most overlooked value that companies bring to the table. What problems can the buyer fix because of your solution? What markets can the buyer now pursue because of the relationship with your company?

  Your ability to empower buyers to go beyond where they are now is real value added. This is as far from commodity selling as you can get. You bring hope and possibilities to the table. Your answers to the questions in the preceding paragraph encourage buyers to dream again about possibilities. Commodity sellers say, "Here's what we do." Value-added sellers say, "Here's what you can now do."

  A missed opportunity is a thorn in the buyer's side. Wouldn't you love to have bought Intel or Krispy Kreme at the initial public offering? What if you could turn back the hands of time and recapture a missed sales opportunity? Hindsight is always twenty-twenty. Selling your opportunity value is selling hope. You solve a problem that has plagued your buyer. You may be able to help buyers capture a missed opportunity or expand their market share into areas they previously couldn't have touched.
- ***Discuss synergy.*** You add value to the buyer's solution through your collective solution. It's the "Intel inside" concept. You can have the

least-known, no-brand-name computer, but when you put a sticker on the front that says "Intel inside," the buyer perceives it to be a quality system. The Intel chip adds value to the computer. How does your solution add value to the buyer's solution? Do you add to the company's product quality, customer response time, or end-user acceptance?

- ***Sell your investment value.*** Buyers perceive your product or service as either an investment or an expense. When buyers perceive it as an expense, they're thinking about all the money leaving the company. When they perceive it as an investment, they're thinking about the money returning to the company. How does your solution represent an investment to each customer?

  Is your solution an investment in product quality, customer satisfaction, or competitive advantage? As an investment, your product or service becomes a value-added solution. As an expense, your product or service becomes a commodity purchase, which brings price sensitivity into the picture. Sell your investment value, instead.
- ***Sell all three dimensions of value.*** You bring a three-dimensional solution to the buyer: product features and benefits, company value-added services, and your commitment to serve. For each buyer need, you offer three levels of benefits: the product, the company, and you. Figure 10.1 displays a planning matrix that you can use to build a three-dimensional solution. It encourages you to ask how the product, the company, and you satisfy each buyer need. Three needs mul-

Figure 10.1 Presentation planner matrix—3-D solution

Need	Company	Product	Sales Rep

tiplied by three dimensions of value equals nine categories of benefits for the customer. The same product from the same company from two different salespeople represents two separate solutions.

- ***Use a value-added work sheet.*** Here's a sales tool that makes it easy for you to quantify the dollar value of your value added to the buyer. Figure 10.2 presents an example. On the work sheet, list your value-added services and what it would cost the buyer to pay for them. Calculate the total value for the whole package. This is positive proof that your value-added solution has a real profit impact on the buyer's situation. You have "tangible-ized" your value added.
- ***Present your value added in a spreadsheet.*** The spreadsheet—your economic value analysis—compares your product or service with that of a competitor by using input variables important to the buyer. This is direct-comparison selling. Include acquisition price, ownership costs, maintenance costs, training costs, disposal costs, and other costs. As Figure 10.3 demonstrates, your acquisition price may be

Figure 10.2 Value-added sheet

Item	Calculated value	Extended value
Electronic Data Interchange (EDI)	Customer usage: 121 times/year @ $35 savings/use 121 × $35 = $4,235	$4,235.00
Safety Training	Two seminars for customer's employees 2 × $1,500 = $3,000	$3,000.00
Profit Enhancement Program	Annual audit of purchasing habits: 2 percent efficiency savings on $120,000 purchase .02 × $120,000 = $2,400	$2,400.00
Equipment Extension of Life Cycle	Six pumps at 12 percent life-cycle extension: 6 pumps @ $15,000 = $90,000 .12 × $90,000 = $10,800	$10,800.00
	Total Value Added Delivered	$20,435.00

Figure 10.3 Economic value analysis

	System A	System B
Acquisition Cost	$ 18,795.00	$ 13,770.00
Annual Energy Costs	$ 675.00	$ 1,405.00
Product Life Cycle	15 years	10 years
Trade-In Value	25%	0
Annual Cost to Own over Product Life Cycle	$ 1,928.00	$ 2,782.00
Trade-In Value	$ 4,698.75	0

higher but your operating costs lower and residual value greater. Thus, your product or service proves to be a better long-term buying decision for the buyer. Buyers who are involved throughout the life cycle of a product understand these comparisons. Buyers call this a value analysis. This is financial selling at its best.

Value-Added Selling Review and Action Points

1. Cutting the distance between the sender and the receiver of a message makes communication more effective and persuasive. When you personalize your message to reflect the buyer's needs, wants, and fears, you make it easier for the buyer to say yes to your solution.
2. Perceived value fuels your buyer's expectations. It is the *context* in which you present your message. When you maximize your perceived value, you put your best foot forward.
3. Performance value demonstrates the profit impact you have on the buyer's business. It is the *content* of your message. While perceived value defines your style, performance value defines your substance.

CHAPTER 11

SERVING

So far, you've learned about focusing and persuading—two of the four major categories of strategies to which value-added salespeople devote themselves. The third major category, supporting, introduces you to the concept of serving and relationship building.

As you begin this supporting phase of the Value-Added Selling process, you are making a shift, ignored in most sales training programs, from offensive to defensive selling. In offensive selling, you're pursuing new business opportunities. In defensive selling, you're protecting existing business. As a salesperson in the offensive mode, you diagnose a problem and prescribe a solution by using your analytical and persuasive skills. As a salesperson in the defensive selling mode, you are more of a logistics specialist who serves customers and seeks ways to strengthen relationships with customers by using your people and promotional skills. The natural outcome of this approach is to grow your existing base of business.

At this supporting phase of the sale, the customer's greatest need is for smooth, seamless, and painless transitions to your solution. The customer wants to work with salespeople who can make this happen. This is the shift point to defensive selling.

In this acquisition phase, you employ two specific strategies to support the customer: serving and relationship building. This chapter is about the support that you provide your customers.

Specifically, I discuss two types of support:

- Process support
- People support

Process Support

This is when you put on your logistics support hat. You've transitioned from sales to service. Your primary job function is facilitator. Your eyes are on the transaction. Your activities parallel the customer's needs. Here is a sampling of these activities and how you add value:

- Verifying order status
- Expediting orders and chasing back orders
- Providing substitute shipments
- Greasing the skids
- Following the supply chain
- Processing credits and returns
- Preparing facilities
- Receiving and warehousing products
- Redistributing goods

To provide the level of support that customers require, you must use your internal selling skills. These are the skills you use to make things happen inside your own company. Working with the credit department to help better serve the customer is internal selling. Convincing the shipping department that packaging flexibility is important to this buyer is internal selling. Selling your manager on the concept of a customer-appreciation golf outing is internal selling. And you thought your job was only to sell to external customers! Internal selling is encouraging and leading your internal team members down the path of complete customer satisfaction.

In this logistics support mode, you follow the order from receipt to delivery, to assure timeliness and accuracy. Likewise, your customers want seamless and painless transitions to your solution. Your job is to make the path smooth.

For example, I know a seller of heavy-duty trucks who is a master of defensive selling. He begins his support by confirming the order to ensure that it is correct. He monitors the progress of the order and provides his customer with periodic updates. When the truck is being prepared for delivery, he conducts a predelivery inspection to ensure that the specifications match the order. When the truck is ready for delivery, he performs a walk-around demonstration to ensure that the buyer understands the truck's operating features. If the buyer has any questions about the documentation or registration, the salesman clarifies that information also. This salesman takes great pride in taking care of his customers. He treats each sale as if it were his first sale with this customer. You can bet it's not his last.

People Support

Now you are wearing your people hat. You're serving people, versus the process. You're a supporter, a champion, a mediator, an ally, a partner, a trainer, and a cheerleader. You're an advocate for the customer and a liaison for your company. You are the customer's safety net, handholder, and therapist all rolled up into one. Your defensive selling activities parallel the customer's needs at this point. You provide value as you serve in the following ways:

- Introducing cross-functional teams to each other
- Training as needed
- Offering technical support
- Fielding inquiries and questions
- Following up on requests
- Providing backup as needed
- Helping to lighten the load

Some people call this the softer support you offer. To the customer, this is as real as it gets. The TLC, hand-holding, and information you provide reassure customers that they made the correct decision in selecting your alternative. This personalized service after the sale is what continues to position you and your company as the value-added solution in the industry. You allay fears and confirm the customer's decision to buy. This eliminates buyer's remorse.

Another salesperson I can cite is a great people supporter. He realizes that during the transition phase, some people at the customer's company may resist the change to a new supplier. He makes it a point to meet those affected by the change and to listen patiently to their concerns. If they require training, he offers his assistance there. He will contact his internal trainers and explain the situation. His concern for people makes his buyer look good and the transition go more smoothly. The heads up he provides to his trainers makes him look good internally, also.

VALUE-ADDED SELLING REVIEW AND ACTION POINTS

1. Serving marks your shift from offensive to defensive selling. The buyer has studied his or her needs and made a purchasing decision from among several alternatives. You demonstrate your commitment to serving by providing logistics and people support.
2. In supporting the acquisition process, you wear a logistics hat. In this mode, you play several roles: expediter, facilitator, and supply-chain manager. Direct your attention to monitoring the demand-and-supply process.
3. Another hat you wear is people support; you support the folks with whom you work. While wearing this hat, you are a trainer, hand-holder, and team leader. As you attend to people issues, you reinforce in the buyer's mind his or her decision to choose your supply alternative.

CHAPTER 12

RELATIONSHIP BUILDING

LIKE SERVING, RELATIONSHIP building is essential to the Value-Added Selling strategy of supporting. Customers, after all, buy more than a product. They buy the whole relationship with the seller. Customers prefer brands, but they reserve loyalty for people.

I was interviewing an association director about the state of customer loyalty in his industry. He told me that the association's researchers discovered that loyalty follows the salesperson. He pointed out that many of the manufacturers in his industry were unhappy with this reality and didn't want to broadcast the finding. The manufacturers wanted to promote brand loyalty.

In a high-tech age, people fear that they will get lost in the shuffle. Selling is relationship management. It's imperative to build strong customer relationships as a foundation for loyalty. And loyalty is a two-way street. It's the reciprocity of trust—the give-and-take of friendship.

Relationship building concerns the dynamics of your one-on-one relationship with a customer. This chapter is about nurturing these long-term, mutually rewarding business relationships.

Specifically, in this chapter I'll discuss:

- Principles of relationship building
- Building a personal relationship with your customer
- Ideas for building business relationships

Principles of Relationship Building

- ***Trust is fundamental.*** Trust is the currency of all great relationships. When two people like each other, trust each other, and want to do business with each other, they will work out the details. And price is generally a detail. Salespeople who deliver on their promises and follow through on customer requests build trust with their customers. Customers know they can depend on these salespeople.
- ***The sale is always about the customer.*** It's their problem. It's their money. It's a solution with which they must live. The sale should be about the customer. What is the focus of your relationship with your customer? Is it more about you, or is it more about the customer? A winning formula for any relationship is to expect 40 percent, and give 60 percent. You'll please yourself and rarely disappoint others.
- ***Empathy is your internal monitor.*** You can be as aggressive as you want in pursuing an opportunity if you balance it with an equally strong measure of empathy. Empathy in this context is perceiving your solution as value received, not just as value added. It requires that you first put the spotlight on your customer. The behavioral side of empathy is asking questions and listening to customers. You must be empathic to understand fully the customer's needs.
- ***Reality is in the eye of the beholder.*** The only reality that matters in selling is in the customer's mind. You may believe that your company delivers great service, and your peers may believe this, too; it's important that you and your peers believe this. But your service is great only when your customer says that it's great. Remember, customer satisfaction is a function of how your solution measures up to others' expectations. If you meet your customers' expectations, you satisfy your customers. If you exceed their expectations, you delight them. It's important that you believe in your service; it's imperative that your customers believe in your service.
- ***Success is a two-way street.*** If I've learned anything in business, it's that your success depends on your ability to help other people succeed. I call this the boomerang effect. You get back what you throw out. Thackeray said, "The world is a looking-glass, and gives back to every man the reflection of his own face." Others may say, "What

goes around comes around." Helping customers achieve whatever they want to achieve is the first step in your achieving what you want to achieve. Value-added salespeople put customers first.

Personal Issues

- ***Listen more than you talk.*** God gave you two ears and only one mouth. He was telling you something. You demonstrate empathy with your ears more than you do with your mouth. Listen to this: Listening is the fundamental selling skill for value-added salespeople.

  Carl Rogers, the father of client-centered therapy, wrote that people fail to listen because of the huge risk they incur in attempting to understand other people. When salespeople listen their way into the customer's world, they risk challenging what they themselves believe, in an attempt to understand fully what the customer is saying. What if the customer is right? It's risky to hear this. However, it's even riskier not to hear this. Denial rarely works. The customer knows how he or she feels. Aren't you curious about those feelings?
- ***Use entertainment.*** Everyone is in a hurry today. Even in my own business, I've noticed I don't make enough time for the social side of selling that I learned as a rookie. Customers are pushed for time also, yet they value this time with sellers. A director of purchasing told me that he likes to use entertainment as a form of getting to know his key suppliers. "I get to see another side of these people. I watch how they treat waiters in restaurants and beer vendors at a ball game. You don't see that in a negotiation. How they treat others outside of my office shows the real person I'm buying from."

  Companies are always looking for ways to cut expenses and trim budgets. Reducing the number of social contacts that salespeople have with customers is not the place to save money. Leave the entertainment budgets alone, managers.
- ***Demonstrate genuine interest in your customer.*** People know when you're a phony. When you give others the floor, make it real. Be truly interested in their welfare. Ask about their families, and listen. Find out what's going on in their lives. Plan to spend time with

them on and off the job. Avoid giving them the bum's rush on a sales call. Let them know that you care about them beyond the order sitting on their desk. Be sincere.

Perform acts of consideration for your customers. Send birthday cards. When the name of a customer's child appears in the newspaper as a result of an accomplishment, send the article and a congratulatory note to your customer. Let your customers know that you care and that you're thinking about them.

- ***Make 'em a hero.*** When I was a chemical salesman, one of my customers told me that my job was to make him a hero twenty-four hours a day, 365 days a year. He said, "Reilly, there's only one reason the Almighty put you on the face of this earth—to make me a hero. You make me a hero, and I'll make you a hero. When the production people call me to ask how I'm able to find this material during a shortage, I'll say, 'Don't worry. I've got you covered.' When accounting asks how I get you to jump through hoops for them, I'll say, 'I'm on it.' Do you get the point, Reilly? Make me look good."

  What a gift! Whatever I did, my job was always to make him look good. It was a crystal-clear mission. I never forgot his admonition and advice. It served me well.

  My customer was a straight shooter. He told me the truth. Somewhat later down the road, the distributor through whom I served this account gave me the help I needed to open my first business.

Business Relationship Ideas

- ***Involve customers in your business.*** Make each of your customers feel like an important member of the family. Ask for their input. Create customer advisory councils. When customers feel as if they are an important part of your business and that you value their opinions, it strengthens the ties that bind you.

  When I was in Houston, I had a customer who worked the first shift in his plant. Perry would stop by our warehouse often on his way home from work. He liked us, and we liked him. He felt like part of the family, and he would occasionally bring his wife. That's involving your customers. I believe Perry felt more at home with us than he did with his own company. Everyone needs to belong somewhere, and we needed Perry as much as he needed us. Do your customers feel as if they belong to your family?

- ***Immerse yourself in their business.*** One of the greatest compliments I have received as a speaker came from an audience member who thought I was an internal trainer for his company. I had spent so much time preparing and tailoring my presentation that it sounded homegrown.

  I've met salespeople who volunteer to work at a customer's business during inventory or during seasonal promotions when the customer needs the extra help. These salespeople send a strong message to customers: that being part of their business is a priority to them.

  My training center is located in a floodplain in Chesterfield, Missouri. During the Great Flood of 1993, I got to see firsthand how supplier salespeople valued their customers' business. When you see a supplier salesperson dressed in jeans and boots, or shorts and a T-shirt, helping fill sandbags or helping clean up after the flood, you'll never forget it. Businesses cannot buy that kind of personal loyalty. Would you fill a sandbag for your customers?

- ***Design customer loyalty programs.*** Loyalty programs encourage customers to return. Frequent-buyer programs, special training seminars, rebates, and bonus-purchase options are just a few examples.

  I shop for my wife at a small specialty jewelry store. Every January, the store sends me a thank-you letter for my business during the previous year. The letter includes a gift certificate proportional to last year's purchases. It's a way for the owner to demonstrate her appreciation for my business while providing an incentive for my repeat business. Do you think that gift certificate pulls in a lot of business for her store?

- ***Deliver proactive service.*** Keep customers ahead of the curve. Take the initiative to nip problems in the bud. Keep your customers out of trouble. A sales rep told me that every Monday morning, she checks her back-order reports for her top customers. She gets updated shipping information on back-ordered items and relays it to customers. She explained, "When I call them, it's service. When they call me, it's a complaint." The real benefit of being proactive is the increased customer satisfaction that results from your efforts.

- ***Help grow their businesses.*** One of the more positive ways to have an impact on your customers' world is to look for ways to help them grow their businesses. This demonstrates your genuine concern for their continued success. This is especially true for small businesses that generally operate with limited resources. Offer growth suggestions. Give them leads. Introduce them to other businesses with which they may develop a supplier relationship. When you help them grow their businesses, you're solidifying your future with them. You've become part of their marketing effort.

Value-Added Selling Review and Action Points

1. Selling is relationship management. Your customers may prefer brands, but they reserve loyalty for people. You can build this strong personal bond with your customers by using your ears more than your mouth. Look for ways to make your customers heroes. They will reciprocate by making you a hero.
2. Building strong relationships with your customers also means seeking ways to help build their businesses. Immerse yourself in your customers' businesses, and pursue ways to help them grow their businesses and run them more efficiently. This helps you to become a valuable resource to customers.

CHAPTER 13

TINKERING

AFTER-MARKETING IS the fourth and final group of strategies that value-added salespeople practice. After-marketing is the sale-after-the-sale. It's nailing shut your back door so that you don't lose business from the back door as fast as you bring it in your front door. There are three after-marketing strategies: tinkering—seeking ways to re-create value; value reinforcement—getting credit for all the value added that your company brings to the table; and leveraging—expanding your business by growing existing customers.

The implicit promise in Value-Added Selling is your pursuit of excellence; in tinkering, you continuously search for ways to re-create value for your customer. Customers want to feel they are dealing with suppliers who want to grow, evolve, and emerge. They want to buy from sellers who are innovative and who put it all together and then push the change curve.

Markets mature. Products develop similar properties. Strategies and services converge. Competitors are constantly seeking ways to close the performance gaps between themselves and the rest of the market. Tinkering means blasting out of comfort zones. It's seeking ways to re-create value for the customer. Tinkering is the behavioral response to your insatiable curiosity about your potential. This chapter is about chasing that potential, pushing the change curve, and putting some distance between you and everyone else in the market. Tinkerers are curious and creative leaders.

Specifically, this chapter treats three principal aspects of tinkering:

- Barrier analysis
- Building better mousetraps
- Making it easier for your customers to do business with your company

The Importance of Tinkering

Tinkering is working as hard to keep the business as you did to get the business. Tinkering is treating your customers as if they were prospects, because they are . . . for the competition. When you tinker, you're doing what a good, quality competitor does to earn the business.

I define tinkering as a positive form of neurosis. It's your benign insecurity over losing the business, coupled with a desperate curiosity about your potential, that keeps you awake at night thinking of ways to get better.

If I were your sales manager and you requested a lower price for an existing customer, I would ask you, "How much tinkering have you done in this account?" Delighted, or even satisfied, customers who believe you are working hard to re-create value rarely complain about price. They complain when you get complacent.

Many salespeople respond to my question by protesting, "That's not fair, Tom. You know how it is in our business. I get busy. I fight a lot of fires. I grease a lot of skids. There's no time to tinker." If there is no time to tinker, how is there time to find new business to compensate for the business you lose?

Value-added salespeople treat their customers well. How would you respond to a customer who asks, "Am I better off being your prospect or your customer?" Sadly, too many salespeople treat their prospects better than they treat their customers.

Barrier Analysis

Tinkering is one part of eliminating the barriers that prevent your company from delivering the kind of world-class service you believe is possible. What gets in the way? I've asked this question of hundreds of employees in a variety of companies, and here's what they've told me:

- ***Negative attitudes.*** These include the attitude that says, in effect, "This would be a great place to work if it weren't for the customer." When employees view serving as a privilege, not a pain, they naturally behave in ways to better serve customers. When employees view serving as a hassle, customers know it because it's obvious in the way these employees interface with customers.
- ***Communication breakdowns.*** Included here are incomplete instructions or a failure to communicate with other employees or with customers. Salespeople may fail to provide inside staff members with the full instructions they need to process specific customer requests.
- ***Mistakes.*** This item always strikes me as ironic. There is never enough time to do something correct the first time, but there is always time to do it over again. Careless mistakes in one's job suggest someone who feels no ownership or pride in his or her work. How do you think customers view these mistakes?
- ***Time constraints.*** In a world that is moving at breakneck speed, lack of time is perhaps the most understandable barrier to providing top-notch service. There is always too much to do and too little time to do it. As with mistakes, there's never enough time to do something right to begin with, but there is always time to do it again.
- ***Lack of resources.*** Salespeople may face shortages of people, money, and equipment. Again, there is too much to do and too few resources to do it. It's difficult to do your job if you don't have all the tools required. Most companies today are working lean, the legacy of downsizing and reorganization. That's one reason why value-added peak competitors see good employees as assets and treat them as if they were gold. They are.
- ***Unrealistic expectations.*** These are primarily the customer's expectations. Someone influenced the customer, a salesperson no doubt, to expect more than what is possible to deliver. Recall our earlier definitions of customer satisfaction and customer delight: customer satisfaction results from meeting your customer's expectations; customer delight is the pleasant surprise of your exceeding their

expectations. A prescription for success in any business is "Promise a lot and deliver more." Create realistic expectations with your customers, and meet or exceed these expectations.

- ***Lack of authority.*** Along with insufficient resources and time, a lack of authority means that employees feel powerless to create the results the customer wants. Part of the problem is management's delegating tasks without delegating the responsibility for the outcome of the work. Another part is a lack of initiative by employees. They do not take ownership.

  I'm familiar with one company that has a simple yet effective problem-ownership policy. If a customer calls you with a problem, it is your problem until your company solves it. You may not have the resources to solve the problem yourself, but you are responsible for seeing that it is resolved. This practice keeps you in the loop and builds accountability. Everyone in this company feels responsible for creating satisfied customers.
- ***Inflexible procedures.*** When employees view policies and procedures as something more than guidelines and rigidly adhere to them, customers hear responses such as, "I'm sorry, sir, that's the way it is. That's our policy." Customers perceive inflexibility. This barrier is generally the result of management's not informing employees that policies and procedures are performance guidelines, not gospel.

A useful tinkering activity is to ask this question inside and outside your organization: "What gets in the way of our delivering the kind of value-added service that we know we can deliver?" Ask employees. Ask customers. Both may know better than you about these barriers.

Asking that question, discovering various barriers, and eliminating them is one way to release your brakes and deliver value-added peak competitor service.

Build a Better Mousetrap

Emerson is attributed with saying, "If a man can write a better book, preach a better sermon, or make a better mousetrap than his neighbor, though he builds his house in the woods the world will make a beaten path to his door." The Japanese call this *kaizen*—an attitude of continuous improvement. Seeking to build a better mousetrap is living the "What if" question. "What if we could do it this way?" "What if we could make our product do this?" Every great product innovation is the evolution of another great idea.

Customers want to feel that you're keeping them ahead of the curve with your innovation. Value-added peak competitors think forward and visualize endless possibilities, stretching their imaginations to their outer reaches.

You can ask the "What if" question throughout your company and with your customers. My first sales job taught me great habits, among them, how to ask for new product suggestions on sales calls. We had to submit three new product suggestions every month. The only way we could do this was to plow the ground by asking the following questions on every sales call: "What would you like to see from suppliers that is not currently available?" and "What would you like to have that you cannot get now?" Even though I worked for one of the oldest companies in the industry, we had some of the most innovative ideas among all competitors in the field.

Make It Easier to Do Business with Your Company

How easy is your company to do business with? Do customers use words such as *inflexible*, *single-minded*, *arrogant*, *indifferent*, and *seller-focused* to describe your policies and procedures? Or, do they use words such as *flexible*, *considerate*, *patient*, *customer-focused*, and *easy to do business with*?

In our value-added survey, buyers told us they wanted to work with sellers who made it easy for them to do business. What can you do to make it easier for your customers to order? How does your credit department perceive its role: does it build bridges to draw people in or build walls to keep the bums out? Are there more convenient ways for your customers to pay for your goods and services? Would special packaging options make it easier for your customers to redistribute your goods and services internally? Can you bundle different product groups more efficiently to reflect special buyer needs?

At the heart of this strategy is an attitude that says, "We can and should look for ways to make it easier to buy and use our products." *Painless*, *seamless*, and *customer-centric* are words that describe the results of your efforts when you tinker to make the customer's life easier.

Even more fundamental is the belief that people continue to grow and develop if they are open to change and humble enough to admit that they aren't finished yet. It's a self-sabotaging form of arrogance to believe that you have no room for growth.

Value-added peak competitors are proud of what they have accomplished, but they balance their pride with an equally strong measure of humility that says, "We're not finished yet. We still have some distance to travel."

VALUE-ADDED SELLING REVIEW AND ACTION POINTS

1. Are you working as hard to keep the customer's business as you did to get the business originally? You must continue to look for ways to re-create value for your customers: tinker. When you tinker, you treat your customers as if they were prospects, because they are . . . for the competition.
2. You tinker as you identify and eliminate barriers to better service. Ask this question inside your organization and of your customers: "What gets in the way of our delivering the type of world-class service we would like to deliver?" The answers to this question will help you direct your attention to areas where you can improve.
3. Being proactive with your service means never having to say you're sorry to the customer. Ask your customers this question often to stay ahead of the curve in serving them: "What would you like us to do differently tomorrow from what we are doing today?" The answers to this question will provide you with direction for improving your solution.

CHAPTER 14

VALUE REINFORCEMENT

MOST COMPANIES WITH which I work bring great value to the table but rarely get credit for everything they do. In most cases, their customers are uninformed about the extent of this value added. You can't fault buyers for taking for granted your added value when they don't know the value of your total solution. The solution is to highlight this value by using value reinforcement.

Like tinkering, value reinforcement is an after-marketing strategy. Value reinforcement means getting credit for what you do. It's a simple principle: The best defense is a great offense. This is the sale-after-the-sale. It's defensive selling at its best.

When customers grow accustomed to receiving value-added services, especially those for which they do not pay directly, they take these services for granted. They expect free services all the time. Suppliers are looking for ways to remedy this situation. Some are now charging for these value-added services. Others are pursuing ways to gain recognition for these services. This chapter is about the latter course—getting credit for what you do.

Specifically, I develop the following topics:

- Documenting your value added
- Value reminding through positive bragging
- Conducting value audits

Documentation

Are you able to attach a dollar value to the services you offer? Can you calculate the profit impact on the customer's business? How much are you really worth to your customers? The answers to these questions provide the backdrop for the financial justification of your solution. Answer these questions, and you'll have your response to "Your price is too high."

Documenting your value-added services is one of the most proactive ways to manage price resistance. I know a sales rep who uses *no-charge invoices* as a way to inform customers of the dollar value of his services. For example, his company once sent two technical people into the field to resolve a problem. After they finished this assignment, the sales rep calculated the expense his company incurred, including travel and field time. He sent the customer a no-charge invoice for $4,400. On the bottom of the invoice, in bold print, he typed, "No charge—part of our value-added service." This was his way of reinforcing his company's value added.

Another client uses a *project savings report*. When the company completes a technical assignment, it sends a recap of the work and its impact on the customer. This report documents the benefits offered by this supplier. It quantifies the impact so that the customer can appreciate the real dollar difference that results.

Warranty reports detail the value of work performed under warranty. Many times, customers misunderstand the cost burden of warranty work. As far as they're concerned, it's free. I experienced firsthand the benefit of documenting this value added when I had a problem with the brakes on my car. The dealer spent two days repairing the problem. The factory reimbursed the dealer for only 1.8 hours. I paid nothing. The service manager showed me the warranty documentation and said, "Just keep us in mind when you need an oil change." This type of communication is especially important for service plans and extended warranties.

Be aware that the service department in many companies plays a vital role in the sale-after-the-sale. The salesperson may sell the first item, maybe a piece of equipment, but the customer's total experience with the company sells the next product or service. That's why Value-Added Selling is a team sport. Everyone is involved.

Customer service action reports, another useful tool, list the situation, the action taken, and the outcome for the customer. One of my clients combines a customer satisfaction survey with an impact statement. After the customer completes side one—the satisfaction survey—the customer estimates the impact of the service on side two. The two-part survey links performance with satisfaction and a positive outcome for the customer, thus reinforcing the company's value to the customer.

Documentation is one way to tangible-ize your value added for the customer. It makes it easy for the customer to see the dollar value of your relationship. It is easier for you to justify your prices against a backdrop of documented value-added services. For example, a ninety-day documentation campaign prior to price increases sets a positive tone for your discussions.

Value Reminding

Value reminding is positive bragging. It's looking for ways to remind customers of everything you do for them. You can't blame customers for raising the price issue if you have failed to remind them periodically of everything you've done for them. For example, when a customer calls you for technical support and you must pass this request along to someone else, you should follow up with the customer to ensure satisfaction. This action demonstrates your concern while reminding the customer of your service.

When I sold through distributors, I prepared a weekly recap of my joint calling activity with my reps, detailing the business we uncovered. I sent this report to my distributor sales manager to remind him that I was adding value to his sales efforts.

If you help a customer secure a piece of business, follow up to see how it benefited the customer. Doing so reinforces that you're working for the customer. Imagine the impact when the customer tells you that your lead resulted in a large sale. You've proved that you're a viable resource. You're part of the customer's sales team.

Testimonial letters also provide a unique way to reinforce your value added. When a customer writes you a testimonial letter, it's to tell you about the great job you've done. More important, the customer is actively remembering the great job you've done. If you want to do something that requires chutzpah in your next proposal to this customer, include a copy of his or her own testimonial letter to you. Who better to remind the customer of your value added than this very same customer?

When you ask a customer for a testimonial quote, print that quote on a page with several other quotes gathered from other customers. Send each customer on the list a copy so that each can see how you've used his or her words. All of these quotes on one page have great visual impact, and this page serves as a value reminder to each customer who reads it.

Value reminding is an activity for everyone in the company. It reflects an attitude that everyone is responsible for reminding the customer of your value added.

Value Audit

The value audit—either formal or informal—is a way to check on your performance with the customer. Formally, it's a customer satisfaction survey. It could be as detailed as the surveys that auto manufacturers use to measure your buying and owning experience. In the customer satisfaction survey, you measure performance and how it produces buyer satisfaction or dissatisfaction.

A supplier performance appraisal recaps your performance, using the list of the value-added services you promised. Use your VIP list (see Chapter 4) as a report card for grading your postsale value added. As you check on yourself, you're reinforcing the value added you provide. It's also a value-reminding exercise.

A value audit could be as informal as asking questions in follow-up visits. "Mr. Customer, I wanted to meet with you today to check on ourselves, to ensure that you're getting all the value on the back end that we promised you on the front end. How are we performing for you?

How can we improve? What would you like us to do for you tomorrow that we didn't do for you yesterday?"

Remember, the best defense is a great offense. By checking on yourself, you're doing what a quality competitor should do when pursuing new business. It's better, however, for you to know your strengths and weaknesses before the competition discovers them.

One of my clients used the value audit concept as a monthly service check. The audit contained a list of questions designed to get in-depth feedback about the company's performance while calling attention to its value-added services, thus combining value reminding with value audits.

Like many defensive selling strategies, value reinforcement is working as hard to keep the business as you did to get the business. It's treating your customers as if they were prospects, because they are . . . for your competitors. You cannot hear this message too often.

VALUE-ADDED SELLING REVIEW AND ACTION POINTS

1. Most companies deliver significant value added for which they never get credit. Are you getting credit from your customers for all of the value added that your company delivers?
2. Seek ways to get credit for your value added by documenting it and surrounding your customers with these value reminders. Positive bragging is letting your customers know everything you do for them above and beyond the call of duty.

CHAPTER 15

LEVERAGING

The average company with which I work could increase its sales in a given year, even if it didn't bring on board one new customer, simply by doing a better job of selling to existing customers. These companies exhibit an incredible preoccupation, bordering on obsession, with finding new business outside of their established bases. In doing so, they ignore opportunities with existing customers. I call this condition "pipeline-itis." An excessive market-share mentality drives this misguided philosophy, which proposes that market share determines profitability.

It takes an average of seven calls to close a prospect on a new idea, compared with three calls to close an existing customer on a new idea. The transaction costs of selling to existing customers are significantly lower than selling to new customers. So, why do salespeople persist in chasing new customers while walking past business in their existing accounts? Either the grass looks greener or their compensation systems reinforce this behavior.

Leveraging is the final after-marketing strategy (joining tinkering and value reinforcement) that allows you to maximize your potential with your existing base of customers. Leveraging is achieving a high ratio of outcome-to-input. It's getting a 150 percent return on 100 percent effort. It's selling deeper and broader into your accounts. This chapter is about leveraging every opportunity—expanding your existing base of business.

Specifically, this chapter treats the following themes:

- Vertical account penetration
- Horizontal account penetration
- Capturing spin-off business

Vertical Account Penetration

Vertical account penetration means selling more products and services to an existing customer. Some people call this concept cross-selling. Some products and services naturally create regenerative pull for other products and services. One product paves the way for the sale of another product. If you sell equipment, then parts and service work are natural cross-sell items. Four of my nine books have the words *value added* in the title. One book naturally pulls sales for my other value-added titles.

When I wrote my book *Crush Price Objections*, I simultaneously recorded an audiocassette album to complement the text. When people called to order the book, my staff read them a one-paragraph description of the complementary product, the album, to generate interest. Fifty-one percent of those who ordered the book also ordered the album! This tandem effort had a dramatic impact on our sales and profitability. Our cost of acquiring additional sales was nil.

Vertical account penetration involves expanding the mix of your products and services. It's increasing the depth and breadth of the things that you sell to a given account. This benefits the customer, also. Customers pay more to place orders with multiple suppliers than with a single source. That's why many customers today seek ways to consolidate their purchases. Your company incurs more transaction costs to sell one or two items to several customers than it does to sell the same total number of items to one account.

On a practical level, customers find it more convenient to buy many items from fewer suppliers. This follows a current trend in purchasing to consolidate purchases. Customers who buy several items from one source are less likely to bounce that supplier if they have a problem. The more levels at which you connect, the stronger the relationship with the customer. The analogy I like to use in my seminars is that trees with deep roots remain steady, even in the most violent storms. Your challenge is to develop rock-deep roots with your existing customers. It's mutually beneficial to consolidate purchases.

Study the product mix in your value-added target accounts. Ask yourself, "What would be the next logical cross-sell opportunity for me?" If you're like most other salespeople, your best potential growth target is an existing customer who buys from many suppliers. Your job is to persuade this customer to consolidate those purchases with your company.

Horizontal Account Penetration

In horizontal account penetration, you're selling additional products and services to other locations and people representing the same account. I learned this practice well as a rookie salesman. I was traveling one day with an experienced distributor sales rep, and we called on a purchasing agent at a petroleum refinery. At the end of the sales call, on our way out, I asked the purchasing agent if there was anyone else in the plant with whom I should speak. The nice thing about being a rookie is that you don't know what you can or cannot ask.

The purchasing agent told me about a small water-testing lab in a remote location that placed its own orders. I thanked him for the lead and asked the experienced rep if he knew anything about this lab. Embarrassed, he admitted that he knew nothing about it. He also mumbled something about an old dog and new tricks.

Never assume that you have all the business. Never assume that customers know everything you sell. Ask these questions: "Is there someone else I should be calling on?" and "Are there other locations of your company that I may call on?" Then ask the customer for a referral into these locations.

Again, the best defense is a great offense. If you discover additional sources of business within the same account, you may be able to protect all of it with a contract that benefits you and the customer. The more of your products and services your customer buys, the fewer opportunities the competition has to sell into the account. It's both an offensive and a defensive strategy. Leveraging locks in the business and locks out the competition. Vertical and horizontal account penetration means selling deeper and wider into your accounts. It's a win-win situation. Both parties benefit by leveraging transaction costs. Customers enjoy the convenience, and you enjoy the extra business. They leverage their buying power, and you leverage your costs.

Capturing Spin-Off Business

Spin-off business is the best way to prospect. It takes the chill out of a cold call. Referral selling is the number one strategy for meeting high-level decision makers. Ask every customer on whom you call, "Is there someone outside your company whom I should meet and get to know?" Take it a step further, and ask your customer to help you arrange the meeting.

My greatest success stories as a salesman, in terms of volume and profitability, were referrals from satisfied customers who paved the way for my introduction to the prospect. I met these prospects as a prequalified supplier. I had credibility that transcended advertising. Word-of-mouth testimony from a trusted friend is still the most effective way to promote.

For the next two weeks, ask your customers this question, and see what happens: "Who should I be talking with?" Leave it that open-ended. Don't limit the leads they give you by adding a qualifying statement such as, "Who should I call who uses what we sell?" Leave your question completely open-ended. Let the customer brainstorm an answer.

A salesperson who recently attended one of my seminars called me two weeks after the program and said, "I asked your referral question twenty times after the seminar and got eleven solid leads, three of which have already turned into sales. I had to quit asking the referral question because I couldn't follow up on all my leads."

Asking for a referral is one of the most basic concepts in selling. When was the last time you did it? Every satisfied customer is a salesperson for you and your organization.

Spin-off business also includes niches. I've heard it said, "In niches, there are riches." This idea means taking what you have learned and using it in another account. Look at your base of business and determine what you have learned. Have you inadvertently or unwittingly carved out a niche for yourself? Have you learned something about selling to a certain group of customers that you could take to the other customers in that niche? Every salesperson specializes in something but may not know it.

VALUE-ADDED SELLING REVIEW AND ACTION POINTS

1. In business there is a dangerous preoccupation with capturing new business. I call this pipeline-itis; companies often ignore profitable and viable opportunities with their existing customers. Are you getting all of the business you should be getting with your existing customers?
2. You can increase your penetration with existing customers in one of two ways: vertical and horizontal account penetration. Seek ways to expand the mix of products you sell to a customer's location or expand the mix of your business by selling to other locations of the same account.
3. Referral selling takes the chill out of the cold call. Who better to open the door for you than a completely satisfied existing customer? Expand your business by asking existing customers for the names of other people whom you could serve.

Part III

VALUE-ADDED SELLING TACTICS

Welcome to the tactical side of Value-Added Selling. I call this the tactical side because in this part I describe the application, or how-to side, of this philosophy. This is where you learn how to execute the value-added philosophy on your sales calls. One of the benefits of Value-Added Selling is its user-friendly philosophy that makes great sense in the classroom and even greater sense on the streets.

The tactical side includes precall preparation, the value-added sales call, and postcall evaluation: You plan. You call. You review. How simple can it get? In theory, it's simple. In practice, it's more challenging.

The value-added sales call model I've designed follows the natural path of everyday conversation as well as persuasion theory. Every conversation has a beginning and an end—a greeting and some parting words. I call this the opening and the closing. Every phone call, letter, E-mail, in-person visit, casual conversation, speech, television commercial, and direct-mail piece has an opening and a closing. There's nothing magical here, just simple communication. The magic is in the middle, the information exchange—probing and presenting.

While probing is the needs analysis, presenting is how you communicate your message to the customer. Value-added salespeople spend most of their time on the sales call probing and presenting—listening to customers and presenting ideas.

In sales, there's an inverse relationship that exists for how you spend your time on a sales call: The more time you invest on the front end probing and listening to buyers' needs, the less time you must spend on the back end closing and resolving objections. Conversely, the less time you spend on the front end probing and listening, the more time you must spend on the back end trying to resurrect a dead sale.

You will notice that in Part III, the heaviest time investment is on the front end—identifying buyers' needs and presenting customized solutions. This is customer-oriented Value-Added Selling.

CHAPTER 16

PRECALL PLANNING

WHEN I ASK salespeople in my seminars how many of them prepare religiously for sales calls, only one hand in ten goes up. Compare that meager response against the fact that 1,500 salespeople and their sales managers rated planning as the most important skill for long-range success in sales! Regardless, precious few do it. The tactical side of Value-Added Selling begins with planning the sales call. You cannot achieve your tactical objectives—in the execution phase—without planning.

Planning means creating the future in your mind, in the present. Planning is your link between dreams and reality. It's outlining the strategy that will help you achieve your dreams or goals. I like to use this formula in my own selling and speaking career: P + P = 2P. Planning and Preparation equals twice the Performance.

After winning the British Open at age twenty-four and becoming the youngest golfer in history to win the sport's grand slam, Tiger Woods was asked by an interviewer how much he practiced. He replied, "If you don't put in the work, you don't deserve the results you want to have." How hard do you work to prepare for a sales call?

Imagine that you're sitting on an airplane, waiting for the doors to shut. The captain announces over the intercom system, "Thank you, ladies and gentlemen, for flying with us. Momentarily, we will close the doors, push back, and taxi out to the active runway. Once we have climbed to our cruising altitude, we will get back with you and inform you of our destination, how long we think it's going to take to get there, and the flying conditions along the route. We will not know any of this until we get up there." Now, that's a new definition of the term *winging it*, isn't it? How long would it take you to get off that airplane?

The preceding example is so ridiculous that most people just laugh it off when I use it in my seminars. And yet, how many times have you made a sales call with that same lack of preparation? No salesperson really plans to fail, but many fail to plan. As a salesperson, are you any less professional than the airline pilot? Of course not, unless you fail to plan.

This chapter is about building your confidence and your competence through better planning.

Specifically, here's what you'll learn:

- Six questions to help you prepare
- The importance of the call planning guide

How to Prepare for Your Sales Call

Call preparation for Value-Added Selling involves three steps: reviewing what you know about the account, asking yourself some call preparation questions, and completing your call planning guide.

Step 1: Study Your Value-Added Target Account Planner

What do you know about this account already? Review the information in your customer file, and bring yourself up to speed with what's happening in the account. The questions from Chapter 5 that I presented for you to study on your VATs are a great precall review. What other sources of information can you tap in your information quest? How about the customer's website, an Internet news service, or your company's files?

You want to seek out opportunity areas with your customers: areas of either pain or desired gain sufficient enough to motivate a change. Study your competitive strengths and weaknesses and how you can make a difference for the customer. Remember, knowledge is empowerment.

Step 2: Ask Yourself Six Questions Before Every Sales Call

If I were your sales coach, I would ask you these six questions before each sales call to help you streamline your efforts and achieve your goals, but since I cannot be with you, I encourage you to ask yourself these questions during call preparation:

1. ***"What do I want to accomplish on this call?"*** Is your objective to gain maximum account penetration, create pull, differentiate your solution, assure customer satisfaction with your solution, reinforce your value-added status, or build a relationship?
2. ***"What do I want to ask the buyer?"*** When conducting your needs analysis, you may want to discover buyer pressure points, uncover opportunity areas, dislodge your competition with target probing, elicit needs-specific responses, or understand the buyer's personal concerns. List your questions in advance to ensure their compatibility with your call objectives.
3. ***"What do I want to tell the buyer?"*** Something about your solution? Something to help sell the buyer on the value-added concept? What specifically do you want to tell the buyer about your three-dimensional solution: the product, the company, and you?
4. ***"What collateral pieces do I need?"*** Do you want to use the VIP list, the Customer's Bill of Rights, a Ten Things to Consider list, a differentiation matrix, the value-added work sheet, the economic value analysis? (Refer to the preparation and usage tips that are discussed in Parts I and II.) Prepare your collateral support pieces before you make the sales call. Place them in a presentation folder to build their perceived value. It's embarrassing to fumble through your briefcase during the meeting with the customer.
5. ***"What obstacles do I anticipate?"*** Will price be a trouble spot? What about buyer apathy or inertia? Has the buyer had a bad experience with us? You can anticipate an objection without creating one. Be ready for buyer resistance: it's a reality in sales. Here's your benchmark for effectively managing price resistance: Whoever is better prepared to deal with the resistance—you or the customer—will emerge victorious from the negotiation.

6. ***Your payoff question, the money question: "What action do I want from the customer at the end of this call?"*** Your action objective for this call is how you will close the sales call. You may want the customer to make a follow-up appointment, agree to the next step in the process, commit to purchasing, give you inventory data, or set up a meeting. How you answer this question is how you will close the sales call. It's a quantitative way to measure your success on the call.

What do you think would happen if you were to ask yourself the foregoing six questions before each sales call? When I ask this question in seminars, you can imagine the responses I hear: "I would increase my sales significantly." "I would be more prepared for the call." "I would feel more in control of the call." or "I would be a professional." If that's the case, why not do it?

Step 3: Complete Your Call Planning Guide

The call planning guide, as shown in Figure 16.1, helps you organize your thoughts for making the sales call. Notice that the call planning guide generally follows the call preparation questions: your objectives, probing, presenting, and closing.

One salesperson asked me in a seminar, "Do I really need to use the call planning guide before every sales call?"

My response was, "No, just for those calls where you want to sell something."

I conducted an experiment with a group of salespeople to determine the effectiveness of the call planning guide. I outlined a cold-call scenario and asked group members how they felt about making the call. On a ten-point scale (with ten indicating a high desire to call and one a low desire), the average score was four. After only a ten-minute pencil-and-paper planning exercise (without further training), the average score jumped to seven. Their confidence level had almost doubled. What do you think that did to their competence level? The participants felt a deeper sense of control because they planned their efforts.

Figure 16.1 Call planning guide

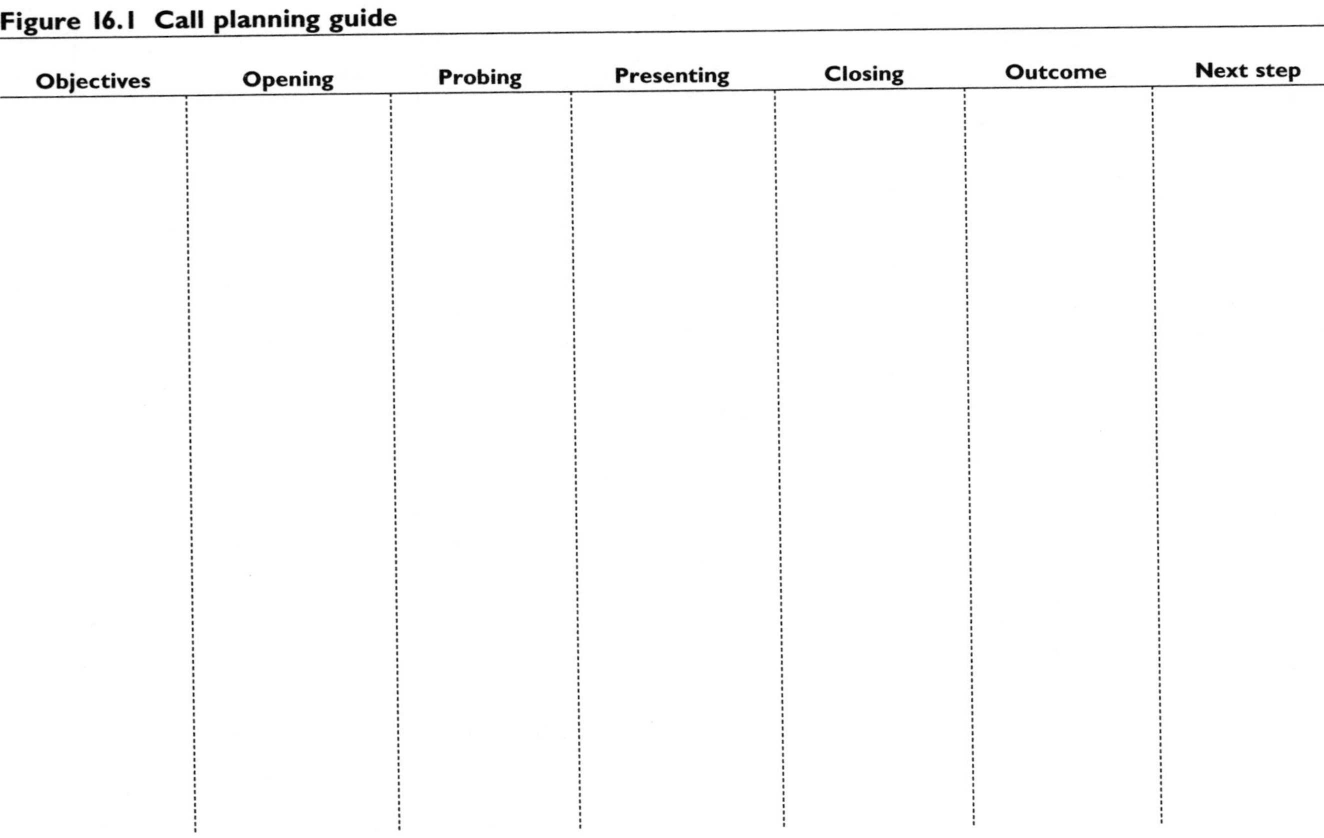

VALUE-ADDED SELLING REVIEW AND ACTION POINTS

1. The most effective and efficient way to increase the probability of your success is through planning. Planning and preparation equals twice the performance. Fewer than 10 percent of your peers plan their sales calls. As you plan your sales calls, you automatically position yourself for success.
2. Plan your sales calls by reviewing what you know about the customer, asking yourself the six precall planning questions, and completing the call planning guide.

CHAPTER 17

OPENING THE SALES CALL

Now that you've planned your sales call, you turn your attention to the first phase in executing the value-added sales call: your opening. Twenty years of sales training has taught me that opening the sales call is one of the greatest weaknesses of salespeople, so opening the sales call presents a great opportunity. You open with impact to get the buyer's full attention.

The opening stage is the first step in your face-to-face meeting with the buyer. You're in the buyer's office, on a job site, or in your showroom. The goal of the opening stage is to get the buyer's attention and set a positive tone for the meeting. I've met few salespeople who do it well. A strong opening is important in all forms of communication.

Newspaper editors always strive for powerful headlines to grab the reader. Book publishers are as interested in a catchy title as they are in a great book. Ad copywriters constantly search for the right hook to snag their target audience. This chapter is about strong openings.

Specifically, here's what I share with you:

- How to open with impact
- How much socializing you should do at the beginning of the call
- Comments to avoid in the early stages of the sale

How to Open

Every strong opening has three components. First, if this is your initial meeting with this buyer, introduce yourself and observe the customary amenities. If you already know the person, exchange courtesies.

Second, explain why you're there. State the purpose of your call. In your call objective, include a benefit for the buyer. The more relevant the benefit, the more quickly you get the buyer's attention.

You have several ways to tell the buyer why you're there, among them:

- Make a positive reference to your product and how it will benefit the company.
- Ask a thought-provoking rhetorical question. Be careful not to sound self-serving with this question.
- Mention a common acquaintance or friend. This referral opening helps establish quick credibility.
- Make a reference to something about the buyer's company.

The third part of your opening is to ask permission to probe. If it's a repeat call, get permission to review. Why? Because it's polite. Also, when the buyer gives you permission to ask questions, it implies a commitment to answer these questions.

There's another reason for you to get permission to probe: justification. A sales manager told me that he had difficulty getting his salespeople to ask questions. They felt that they were being intrusive. By teaching them the permission technique, the sales manager alleviated their reluctance; his salespeople said they no longer felt as if they were prying. Learning to ask permission affected their attitudes about probing. They were more open to it.

The following sample openers demonstrate how this technique sounds when you put it all together:

(Cold call)

"Good morning, Mr. Spence. I'm Frank Harris with Modern Research Labs. It's a pleasure to meet you. As I mentioned in our phone conversation earlier this week, the reason I wanted to meet with you today

is to discuss the unique bundle of timesaving, value-added services that our company has created specifically for companies that operate in your niche. There are many things that I could tell you about us, but I'd like to hear more about your company. May I ask a few questions?"

(Repeat call)

"Good morning, Jill. It's great to see you again. (At this point, exchange pleasantries.) The last time we met, you told me about a computer glitch that is wreaking havoc in production planning. Is that still an issue? (Pause for response.) What would it mean to you if I told you our engineers have come up with a possible solution? (Pause.) Before getting into that, I need to review a couple of things. Do you mind if I ask a couple of questions?"

(Repeat call)

"Brad, it's a pleasure to meet with you. Our mutual friend, Brendan, gave me your name and suggested we meet. We've worked with his company for the past three years and are responsible for creating his last ad campaign, which took the market by storm. That's why I wanted to meet with you today—to see if we could create the same kind of results for your company. May I lead with some questions?"

In each of those opening statements, the salesperson flirted with a benefit for the buyer: offering a unique bundle of timesaving, value-added services; solving a critical problem; and creating amazing marketing results. The salesperson gave the buyer a reason to listen: it benefited him or her. It made sense for the buyer to listen. And in each case, the salesperson got permission to probe.

Guidelines for Socializing

This question surfaces often in our seminars: "How much socializing should I really do with the customer?" A simple rule of thumb is to take your lead from the customer, who will let you know how much socializing is appropriate. A big mistake salespeople make is in assuming that the best way to build rapport with buyers is to engage in small talk.

One study of buyers found that unsolicited small talk was their number one irritant. The study concluded that the best way to open the sales call is to tell the buyer why you're there, announce your call objective, and state your intention.

Take your lead from the customer. Some buyers are social, while others are more formal. Social buyers are people oriented, which affects both the context and the content of the sales call. With these buyers, the context of the call is relaxed and social. Getting to know you as a person is a big part of the process for the people-oriented buyer. Similarly, the content of the sales call primarily reflects people issues: training, support, ease of use, safety, morale, and similar concerns. It's important for you to frame your solution within the context that reflects the buyer's priorities—in this case, people.

Other buyers are task oriented. The context of this sales call is thus formal and businesslike. These buyers generally want to get to business quickly. You demonstrate your competence early by getting down to the task at hand. For content, they prefer to hear about performance, productivity, operational and functional characteristics, profitability, and other quantifiable benefits. If these buyers socialize, it's at the end of the call, after they have completed the task. Then they may relax their guard and give you a peek at the person.

Mirroring your buyer's priority—task orientation or people orientation—is one way to establish credibility. Another way to build credibility and trust is to pace the buyer. Some people move quickly and intuitively. Other people are methodical and analytical. Potential conflict arises when you move at your pace versus the buyer's pace. You can reduce the psychological distance between you and the buyer by mirroring his or her priority and pace. You run into problems when you impose your priority and pace on the buyer.

Comments to Avoid

Over the years, I've collected many opening comments from salespeople, and some of them read like a list of what not to do on a sales call, for various reasons. Using them demonstrates a lack of confidence in yourself or your product, a feeling that you may be wasting the buyer's time or setting a negative tone for the call. Avoid the following openers:

"I was just in the area visiting another customer and thought I would stop by to see you." You're really saying that this buyer isn't special enough to warrant a separate call. You've made this buyer an afterthought, a time filler between other, more important appointments.

"I know you're busy, and I promise not to take up a lot of your time." You sound like a time waster. This approach automatically relegates you to that status. Buyers feel contempt for people who waste their time. Is that really how you want to position your visit with this customer?

"You probably weren't much interested in doing anything today." A salesman actually approached me this way one day. He walked into my office, smiled weakly, and said, "You're probably the least-likely candidate today to buy a long-distance service." I said, "You're right!" He didn't want to sell, and I didn't want to buy. We got along famously. He was bland and obviously unconvinced that his product was worth my time.

"I've heard through the grapevine that your company has had some problems in this area." Now your buyer is suspicious; who's talking about him or her in the marketplace? Suspicion and paranoia are not the emotions you want buyers to feel when you're attempting to build trust and rapport.

"Would you be interested in saving money?" Questions such as this one are too obvious and self-serving. Buyers say in surveys that they reject obvious questions or questionable benefits such as, "We can cut your costs in half."

VALUE-ADDED SELLING REVIEW AND ACTION POINTS

1. A strong opening—the attention getter—is an integral part of communication. All persuasion begins with getting the attention of the receiver of the message. Develop a strong opening statement to begin your value-added sales call.

2. Take your lead from the buyer. Some buyers prefer to socialize; other buyers prefer to get down to business. Your sales approach should mirror the buyer's preferences. You reduce the distance between buyer and seller when you respect the buyer's priorities.

CHAPTER 18

THE NEEDS ANALYSIS STAGE

IMAGINE THAT YOU'RE in your doctor's office. The doctor is describing a new medication for diabetes patients, extolling the virtues of this revolutionary drug. It is readily available and offers patients an annual savings of 50 percent over standard insulin. Obviously, your doctor is excited about this new product. The doctor writes a prescription for you. You're confused because you're there for a flu shot. Moreover, you don't even have diabetes! The doctor has prescribed without diagnosing your symptoms.

How many times have you done to a buyer what the doctor has done to you? Many salespeople make calls in which they detail their product, assuming that the buyer needs it and is aware of this need. You can't assume that. To sell value added, you must first analyze the buyer's needs thoroughly. This is the essence of the customer value focus.

For you, the value-added salesperson, the needs analysis represents the next step in executing the value-added sales call. This is your way of pinpointing the customer's needs so that you don't prescribe without diagnosis. This chapter is about developing your probing skills.

Specifically, I take the following course in this discussion:

- Define the needs analysis
- Suggest how to ask questions effectively
- Demonstrate three questioning areas
- Explain conceptual selling
- Examine how you can become a better listener

What Is the Needs Analysis?

The needs analysis is a communicative fact-finding mission. It's a full-blown exploration into the buyer's needs, wants, desires, and fears. It's an in-depth examination and assessment of all the variables that may influence the buying decision. You gather data and consider the buyer's perception regarding the identified needs. This is the behavioral side of customer-izing. It is the most important phase of the sale because it enables you to correctly prescribe the right solution for the buyer's problem.

By thoroughly analyzing the buyer's needs, you help the buyer objectively understand specific needs. This objective awareness raises the buyer's constructive pain level with the status quo. Your strategic questioning often acts as a catalyst, allowing buyers to realize their dissatisfaction with their current ways of attempting to meet their needs. Dissatisfaction drives change.

You're digging for root-canal pain. The premise is that usually only one thing—excruciating pain—motivates someone to go through a root canal. That pain must be so intense that it hurts too much to do nothing. This is what you're probing for in the needs analysis. Root-canal pain causes buyers to change. People change when the disadvantages of doing nothing exceed the advantages they would realize from doing something—in short, the current pain is greater than the current gain. When their current situation hurts more than it helps, buyers open up to change. Probe deep. Find the root-canal pain.

Probing for buyer needs unearths the nonprice variables that affect the buying decision. Getting the prospect to elaborate on the importance of these nonprice variables mitigates the role of price in the buying decision. Many times, customers are unaware of these variables until someone asks about them.

Management studies tell us that involvement in the change process builds commitment and lowers resistance to new ideas. Involving the prospect via questioning breaks down resistance to change and builds commitment. When you couple an objective awareness of one's situation with this active involvement, the motivation to change comes from within the individual. The prospect wants to change, and that makes your job easier.

Once you get the buyer involved, raise his or her objective-awareness level, and create an internal motivation to change, the buyer is more eager to buy than you are to sell. What does that do to your closing ratio? Do you think price plays a major role in the buying decision if the buyer's desire to own your product is greater than your desire to sell? No way! Price instead assumes the position it richly deserves—only one of many buying criteria, rather than the main reason someone buys a product.

Think of this probing technique as icing on the cake. When you probe, you're telegraphing strong messages to your prospect. You're saying, "I care enough to listen—to invest part of my life to hear your problems." This message builds trust and rapport. It also differentiates you from all other salespeople who call on that buyer and deliver canned presentations. You're recording a strong, sincere message on the tape inside the buyer's head.

The prospect thinks, "This person cares enough to listen to my concerns, understand my problems, and commit to a viable solution for them. This salesperson is different from most others who've called on me. I want to do business with this rep because I trust this person."

The premise is simple. If two people want to do business with each other because of trust and rapport, the details (such as price) rarely block the sale. If the buyer trusts you and feels comfortable with you because you genuinely care, price is not on the radar screen. The buyer trusts that your price is fair and reflects equity in what he or she is paying and receiving.

By performing the needs analysis, you communicate: "It's OK to pay more for the value we offer. We understand your problems and share your concerns. We're committed to finding a solution that makes sense for you." The needs analysis enables you to customize your solution for the buyer, and who doesn't want a customized solution?

Not performing a needs analysis leaves you with few options. You regurgitate a canned presentation because you're clueless about what's most important to the buyer. When you fail to ask questions, you miss an opportunity to build trust and rapport.

Mechanics of Questioning

To conduct an effective needs analysis, you must have a thorough understanding of the mechanics of asking questions. You must know how to construct questions that draw the information you desire. When designing your questions, consider these three areas: length of response, intent, and bias.

Open and Closed Questions

Your first consideration in formulating questions is how lengthy a response you want and need. An open-ended question encourages the respondent to elaborate. The question generally requires a lengthy response. The chief advantage of the open-ended question is that the buyer volunteers additional information and explains his or her position more thoroughly. It builds commitment because of customer involvement. A disadvantage of an open-ended question is that the response is time consuming, and you may lose some conversational control.

Typically, open-ended questions begin with *Why*, *How*, *What*, *Tell me about*, or similar words or phrases designed to gain active participation. A facial expression also is an open-ended question if it encourages the other person to respond freely. Here are some examples of open-ended questions:

- Why do you feel that way?
- What are your main concerns in buying?
- Tell me about your business.
- How do you feel about dealing with more than one supplier?
- Why is price important in your decision process?

Closed-ended questions, on the other hand, elicit a short response—generally one or two words. You intentionally limit the response length.

Closed-ended questions offer two major advantages: they give you greater conversational control, and they are more time efficient. The primary disadvantage is that the respondent rarely offers unsolicited information. Another disadvantage is that consecutive closed-ended questions sound like an interrogation, not an interview. Don't machine-gun buyers with closed probes, because it will shut down the dialogue.

Generally, closed-ended questions begin with words such as *When*, *Who*, *Which*, *Where*, *How many*, *How much*, *Do you*, *Are you*, or *Will you*. Notice that the following examples of closed-ended questions have one thing in common—they evoke a short response:

- How often do you order these items?
- Which of these do you prefer?
- When do you place orders?
- Have you had problems with your current supplier?

You can get the same information by asking your question as either open-ended or closed-ended. For example:

- What role does price play in your buying decision? (open)
- Is price important in your buying decision? (closed)

Again, the open-ended question encourages a lengthier response. One advantage in the example just cited is that the prospect may tell you *why* price is so important. You can dig for information both ways—open or closed. Ideally, you should ask all open-ended questions. Realistically, you may need to ask a few closed-ended questions to regain conversational control or to confirm what you heard from the lengthy response. For example:

- What are your major concerns in purchasing? (open) (Pause for a lengthy response.)
- Then, price and delivery are your two major concerns? (closed)

Use this rule of thumb to encourage buyers to respond freely: Eighty percent of your questions should be open-ended. If the conversation meanders, ask a closed-ended question to regain control quickly.

People often ask me in seminars, "How do I get the silent type to open up?" I advise them to examine the nature of the questions they ask their buyers. Asking too many closed-ended questions inhibits buyer participation. Keep your questions open-ended to encourage full buyer involvement.

Direct and Indirect Questions

The second consideration in designing questions is your intent. How obvious do you want to be with your questions? How blunt and straightforward can you afford to be?

A direct question is blunt, straightforward, and to-the-point. There is no doubt what you're asking. It's obvious. An advantage of the direct question is that there is no confusion about the information you want. Plus, it may be more time efficient. A strong disadvantage of the direct question is that it's generally offensive and threatening. Here are three examples of direct questions:

- Do you have the authority to make this decision?
- Is price important to you?
- Why do you buy from that supplier?

There is a strong element of risk in these questions because they are so blunt. In most cases, it's prudent to soften the delivery and minimize the perceived threat. Do this by using an indirect question instead.

An indirect question veils your intent. It's a roundabout way of getting the same information. Since it's not as threatening as the direct question, the indirect question is easier to answer. Because it is a low-risk question, you're more likely to get a response. In fact, the indirect question encourages the other person to volunteer additional information. A disadvantage is that it may not be as time efficient because what you're asking isn't as obvious. Here are three examples of indirect questions:

- How does your buying procedure work?
- What things are important when making a buying decision?
- Do you have more than one supplier?

Notice that these questions parallel the three direct question examples. In the first indirect question—"How does your buying procedure work?"—I give the prospect an opportunity to save face, because I don't question the person's buying authority. I ask how the buying process works in general. It offers the buyer a chance to volunteer the fact that he or she is or is not the decision maker. I get my information in a nonthreatening manner.

In the second example, I don't call attention to the price issue. I ask about all things that are important in this decision. It raises the buyer's awareness that there are considerations other than price. I don't assume that price is the only criterion. If price is important, I still find out with the answer.

With the third question, I ask how many suppliers the buyer has. My intent is to get the buyer talking about all suppliers. This way, I can discover what I really want to know: why this buyer purchases from a given supplier. It's a roundabout way of getting the information, but the buyer may be more open to the indirect approach.

The best time to use an indirect question is when you feel that the nature of the question is risky and warrants some caution. In such cases, broach the topic indirectly to get your information. If you perceive limited risk, ask the question more directly.

Window Exercise

You can combine intent with length of response and, thereby, ask for the same information four ways. Think of the flexibility this gives you! Figure 18.1 provides examples.

This exercise builds your flexibility in asking questions. You minimize risk and reduce the perceived threat by moving from direct-closed (quadrant 2) to indirect-open (quadrant 3).

Figure 18.1 Window exercise

	Open	Closed
Direct	Tell me about your involvement in the buying decision. What role does price play in your final decision to buy?	Do you have the authority to make this decision? Is price your main concern?
Indirect	How are these buying decisions normally made? What things are important when you make your buying decision?	Is there a standard way of making these buying decisions? Do you have something that is most important when making your buying decision?

	Open	Closed
Direct	1 Moderate Risk	2 Greater Risk
Indirect	3 Least Risk	4 Lower Risk

Make a list of all the questions you'd love to ask your buyer. Select the most threatening questions, and use the window exercise to soften them. Watch the reaction of your buyer when you ask these indirect-open questions. The buyer will volunteer more information than you anticipated. By constructing these low-risk, nonthreatening questions, you will make it easier for the buyer to respond.

Leading and Neutral Questions

The third area to consider when designing your questions is bias. Do you want an objective, fact-based response, or do you want the buyer to echo what you ask? Do you want the prospect to speak freely or just agree with you? Do you want to ask questions that encourage dialogue, or do you want to ask questions that lead the other person?

Your objective in the needs analysis is to engage the buyer and open him or her up in order to gain maximum information. Leading questions discourage this give-and-take environment. A leading question suggests the answer you desire. It leaves no room for the buyer to voice opinions.

A neutral question, on the other hand, offers no suggestion of what the response should be. It doesn't lead, so the other person doesn't feel threatened.

Here are examples:

- Is price important? (neutral)
- Price is important, isn't it? (leading)
- Are you the decision maker? (neutral)
- You are the decision maker, aren't you? (leading)

A leading question tends to make buyers feel defensive, because it forces a response. How do you feel when someone uses leading or biased questions on you? If you're like most people, you resent others telling you what to think and say. You feel cornered, manipulated, and controlled—none of which is conducive to building rapport or gaining information.

Sales trainers who advocate the use of leading questions in this phase of the sale mislead you. They're encouraging you to use techniques on others that you would resent someone for using on you. There is an inconsistency here. Salespeople don't use skills that are philosophically incongruent with their own beliefs. Avoid bias in your questions during the needs analysis. Remember, your objective is to gather facts, not elicit canned responses.

Strategic Questioning Areas

In addition to knowing *how* to formulate your questions, it's equally important for you to know exactly *what* to ask. The purpose of this section is to show you how to arrange your questions. Asking questions in the order that I present in this section will help you to capitalize on the logic of the needs analysis. Divide your questions into these three categories: situational, competitive, and projective questions.

Situational Questions

Situational questions elicit information about the customer's world: goals, wants, needs, decision process, and so forth. The buyer gives you information regarding all of those variables that influence the buying decision. Subdivide your situational questions into two groups: general information and specific need.

General Information Questions

General information questions are global, broad-based, nonthreatening questions that spark the conversation and provide a useful backdrop for focusing on the buyer's world, specifically the following five aspects of that world: industry, customer base, company, competition, and personal. The following general information questions exemplify each of the five aspects:

- Tell me about your marketplace. (industry)
- What trends do you see in your market? (industry)
- Who are your customers? (customer base)
- What do your customers want from you? (customer base)
- Who is your competition? (competition)
- What competitive pressures do you face? (competition)

- How does your decision process work? (company)
- How long has your company been in this market? (company)
- How long have you been with the company? (personal)
- How does this decision affect you personally? (personal)

Notice that these questions are nonthreatening and serve as good conversation starters. You may not need to ask as many as I have listed here. At least, you want to ask, "Tell me about your business."

Specific Need Questions

Here, you ask for the prospect's needs, wants, requirements, and expectations from a product, a supplier, and a salesperson—the three dimensions of value. Get the necessary information to determine whether your company and product are a good match for your buyer's needs. Ask questions about specifications and delivery dates. Determine budget limitations. Probe for the buyer's quality needs. Ask questions in all three dimensions of value. For example:

- What are you looking for in a supplier? (company)
- What kind of technical support do you need on this project? (company)
- What availability does your project require? (product)
- What product specifications do you need? (product)
- What do you expect from me as your salesperson? (salesperson)
- How will you measure my effectiveness as your rep? (salesperson)

You are asking, "What do you need?" Situational questions make it easy for you to initiate the sales conversation. They are rapport building, nonthreatening, and fact oriented. You're asking the prospect to elaborate on his or her needs, wants, and fears.

Competitive Questions

Following situational questions, competitive questions are the second major category of needs analysis questions. Answers to competitive questions give you information about your competitors and how well they perform for this buyer.

How-Met Questions

How-met refers to how buyers meet their needs—via your competition. The competition could be a past, current, or future supplier. It could also be an in-house solution that the buyer uses. Here are two examples of how-met questions:

- How do you currently handle your sulfuric acid needs?
- Who is your current supplier for sulfuric acid?

How-met questions help you identify your competition for a specific customer.

How-Well Questions

How-well questions are performance oriented. You're seeking information about the competition's performance. You want to determine what the buyer likes and dislikes about the current supplier as well as the competitor's goods and services. Are this supplier and product meeting the buyer's needs satisfactorily? The following are examples of how-well questions:

- How well does your current supplier meet your needs?
- What's been your experience with the sulfuric acid you're using?
- What type of feedback have you received from your people about this material?

Your objective is to raise the buyers' awareness level concerning their current way of attempting to meet their needs. In doing so, you want the buyer to realize that the competitor's solution may fail to satisfy those needs. Avoid anything that may be viewed as sour-grapes selling, such as bad-mouthing the competition. Remember that the buyer made the decision to use that supplier. Walk softly with your competitive probes. At the same time, you do want to provide an accepting climate for the buyer to voice concerns about current problems. Create a listening opportunity for the buyer to discuss the problems that other suppliers have caused. Ask about the impact these problems have had on the buyer's world.

Projective Questions

Projective questions follow situational and competitive questions to make up the final group in the needs analysis stage. Your intent with projective questions is to highlight the gap between the buyer's needs and how he or she attempts to meet these needs. This group of questions comprises two subgroups—ideal questions and the impact question.

Ideal Questions

Ideal questions are hypothetical, or "What if," questions. Encourage the buyer to dream by taking a trip to Fantasy Island in order to consider the ideal buying solution. Ask buyers about what changes or improvements they would like to make in how they are attempting to meet their needs. Following are some examples:

- If you could change anything about your current supplier, what would you change?
- What would be your notion of the ideal product?
- What would you like to see us do for you that your current supplier is not doing?
- If you were a supplier, what would you do differently?

In each case, you've asked the buyer to dream about the ideal solution to a problem.

The Impact Question

Take the ideal question one step further and ask what effect the stated changes would have on the buyer's business: "If you could improve something about the service level you're receiving currently, what would you change? How would that help your business?" This is the impact question.

The impact question encourages the buyer to elaborate on *why* he or she should change current suppliers. The beauty of this question is that the buyer does all the selling and convinces even you that there may be a better mousetrap. The next logical comment from the prospect is, "What do you have available that could give me the things I need?" Now the buyer is open to change, and your task is to demonstrate how your solution can be the answer.

Regarding this tactic, I'm often asked in my seminars, "What happens if the buyer can't think of any changes or improvements to make? What do I do at that point?" You suggest ideas and get a reaction to them. The ideas you suggest are coincidentally the unique strengths your company offers. The following scenario demonstrates how to do this:

Seller: "Mr. Buyer, if you could change one thing about your current supplier, what would that be and how would it affect your business?"

Buyer: "I'm not sure I'd change anything. We're happy with what we have right now."

Seller: "Let me suggest a couple of ideas and get your feedback. How would you improve the delivery time and technical support from your current supplier?"

In this example, you draw attention to delivery and technical backup. Narrow your suggestions to two specific areas for the prospect to address. It's up to the prospect to tell you about some desired changes in these areas. By admitting that there are some needed improvements in these areas, the prospect opens the door for your presentation. Then, describe the features and benefits of your delivery and technical support.

If you scrutinize the logic of the needs analysis, you discover how amazingly simple it is. You're asking three basic questions:

- What are your needs? (situational)
- How are you meeting those needs? (competitive)
- How can we better address those needs? (projective)

Strategic Objectives

Forming strategic objectives allows you to put the needs analysis in motion as you ask questions in each of the three probing areas: situational, competitive, and projective. You can use the needs analysis, for example, to sell against price. You begin with strategic questioning objectives, determining what you want to accomplish with your questions. One strategic questioning objective is to gather facts. A second objective is to sell your uniqueness. By asking the right questions of the buyer, you plant seeds in the buyer's mind for a potentially better mousetrap. Your questions spotlight areas where the buyer could find a better solution for root-canal-type problems.

By probing with strategic questioning objectives, you preempt the price. You minimize its importance and underscore all variables a buyer must consider when purchasing. You might design the following questioning scenario for a sales call. Notice I begin with a strategic questioning objective. This adds a sense of purpose to the questions.

Strategic objective: To gather facts and plant seeds regarding our value added (our strong technical department support).

Situational Questions: "What are your needs?"

How often do you find yourself in the position of needing additional technical support?

Given the complexity of your process, how involved do a supplier's technical people need to be in your operation?

I understand that many of your jobs are custom work. What do you need from a supplier in terms of customization?

Competitive Questions: "How are you meeting these needs?"

How have you handled your needs for customization and technical support in the past?

What problems have you encountered in getting the support and flexibility you need?

Projective Questions: "How can we better address these needs?"

If you could improve the technical support and degree of customization you've received in the past, how would you change them?

What effect would that have on your business?

Armed with information gathered from your needs analysis probing, you're able to advance to the presentation stage, which is where you tell your story. Naturally, you tell how your technical support and ability to customize can satisfy the buyer's unmet needs. You sell proactively against price by highlighting important buying criteria that eclipse the acquisition price. This mitigates the importance of price by raising other relevant issues. Realistically, you have not eliminated the price issue totally, but if you arrange your questions around a strategic objective, you relegate price to its proper perspective: only one of many variables to consider.

Summarize Needs

Once you have thoroughly analyzed the buyer's needs, you should summarize your understanding of these needs in your own words. Feed back your understanding to the buyer for confirmation. When you summarize buyer needs, several things happen. First, you're demonstrating that you were listening and that you understand the situation. Second, you're verifying your understanding of the buyer's specific needs. Third, you're building commitment by getting the buyer to agree to the needs you've uncovered.

When summarizing, begin with a simple lead-in phrase and then recap what you've learned about the buyer's needs. When you get agreement to these needs, use it as a springboard to transition to the presentation stage. For example: "Ms. Buyer, based on our conversation, I understand that you need better lead time, tighter quality control checks, and more flexible shipping hours. Does this cover it? (Yes.) Let's look at some ways that we can help you achieve these objectives!"

Tips for Questioning

Begin by asking permission to probe. It's courteous, and the buyer commits to answering your questions. For example, "Would you mind if I asked a few questions to better understand your business?"

- Ask one question at a time.
- Ask open-ended questions most of the time.
- Ask indirect questions to reduce a perceived threat.
- After you ask a question, pause to allow time for a response.

- Take brief notes. (You may even want to ask permission to do this.)
- Begin your needs analysis with a questioning objective. Know why you're asking questions.
- If you sense that the other person has a problem in a specific area, pursue it with a follow-up probe. Dig deeper.
- Interview; don't interrogate. You're not there to fill out a questionnaire. Your goal is to get the other person talking about problems.
- When constructing your needs analysis, make sure that you ask questions in each of the three strategic questioning areas: situational, competitive, and projective.

Active Listening

Asking questions is half of the communications formula. The other half is listening actively to what the other person says. Active listening is not passive hearing. Active listening is inputting what the person says, processing it, and feeding back relevant information. As an active listener, you are busy processing information and adding to the conversational momentum.

Barriers to Effective Listening

Listening sounds easy, doesn't it? It can be, if you focus. When you submit to distractions—internal or external—listening is difficult. Let's see how many of these barriers you recognize!

- Daydreaming—your mind is in the Bahamas
- Narrow-mindedness—you, alone, have all the answers
- Facts-only listening—the other person's nonverbal messages and conversational nuances escape you
- Time pressure—you feel rushed
- Outside noise—you yield to distractions around you
- Internal noise—you're somewhere inside your head instead of in the conversation

- Information overload—you're overwhelmed with too much input from the other person
- Techno-talk—you're lost (even worse, your customer is lost) in a sea of technical jargon

I believe that risk is the number one barrier to effective listening for salespeople. If salespeople actively listen to buyers, they risk agreeing with a buyer's point of view that may differ significantly with the salesperson's call objective.

Carl Rogers said it best: "To be effective at all in active listening, one must have a sincere interest in the speaker. Active listening carries a strong element of personal risk. If we manage to accomplish what we are describing here—to sense deeply the feeling of another person, to understand the meaning his experiences have for him, to see the world as he sees it—we risk being changed ourselves. It is threatening to give up, even momentarily, what we believe and start thinking in someone else's terms. It takes a great deal of inner security and courage to be able to risk one's self in understanding another."

Irritating Listening Habits

Do you ever find yourself engaged in any of these actions while in conversation?

- Finishing someone else's sentences—putting words in the person's mouth
- Prejudging the speaker because of your bias
- Interrupting the speaker to inject your opinion
- Looking away toward something or someone else—splitting your attention
- Jumping to conclusions before the other person finishes
- Rushing the speaker—verbally or nonverbally dismissing the person
- Stealing the spotlight with one-upmanship
- Using poor posture—slouching or displaying condescending body language

Becoming a Better Listener

When you listen actively to your customer, the focus is exactly where it needs to be: on the speaker. You're engaged, and so is the other person. When buyers participate in the sale, they buy. The tips presented here will help you do a better job of listening to your buyer.

- ***Don't interrupt.*** As basic as this sounds, buyers can't talk if you're constantly interrupting. Let others complete their thoughts and their sentences before you respond. It's annoying to have others finish sentences for you. It's also rude to presume you know what someone else would like to say.

  Aggressive sales types naturally want to move the conversation along. However, you'll discover that listening your way to success is a lot more fun for everyone. Be courteous. Be polite. But mostly, be quiet.
- ***Practice silence.*** Avoid responding too quickly to the buyer's questions. By the same token, after you ask a question, remain silent and let the other person take time to consider a response. Silence can be intimidating—that's why salespeople have trouble using it effectively. As you practice patient and silent listening, you'll be amazed at what others tell you.
- ***Take notes.*** When you write down what a buyer says, it directs your attention and also demonstrates that the person's words are important to you. Informing people beforehand that you plan to take notes of your conversation makes them less defensive. Develop your own shorthand for taking notes with customers.
- ***Clarify.*** When you're unsure about something said to you, clarify. Ask why, or probe to be sure that you fully understand. Clarifying demonstrates that you're paying attention and you care enough to understand fully what you're hearing. Simply say, "Could you be more specific, please?"
- ***Restate.*** Periodically restate what the other person says. This demonstrates that you understand and that you're operating on the same level, the same page, as the customer. For example, "So, what you're saying is . . . ."

- ***Summarize.*** Throughout the conversation, summarize key points to demonstrate that you've heard correctly. Summarizing also serves to refocus a conversation that has meandered: "Let me be sure I understand where we are . . . ."
- ***Listen nonverbally.*** Watch the customer's nonverbal signals. Are the nonverbal questions open or closed? Do these nonverbal signals move toward you, engaging you? Does your buyer withdraw with his or her nonverbal signals—moving away from you? To demonstrate active listening, lean forward, nod, and use verbal reinforcement to accompany your nonverbal responses, indicating to the buyer that you're actively engaged in the conversation.
- ***Use confirmation statements.*** You can add momentum with an occasional "Uh-huh," "Mmm," "I hear you," "You bet," or "That's an interesting point." Verbal reinforcement, along with attentive nonverbal responses, will demonstrate the impact that the speaker is having on you.

So, what is the greatest skill a salesperson possesses? It's the ability to communicate with customers: to ask questions that cause buyers to think, and to listen actively to what buyers have to say. You must master this skill to be successful in sales.

Value-Added Selling Review and Action Points

1. The needs analysis stage is your fact-finding mission to direct buyers' attention to their total needs, wants, and fears. As you ask more questions and actively listen to the buyer, you develop an in-depth understanding of how you must customize your solution to this person's buying position.
2. Your questions will be either open-ended or closed-ended. Ask more open-ended questions than closed-ended questions when your objective is to draw the other person deeper into the conversation and encourage him or her to respond freely.

3. When soliciting information about a buyer's needs, probe in three specific areas: use situational questions, which give you information on the buyer's expectations; competitive questions, which provide information on how the buyer is attempting to meet these needs; and projective questions, which spotlight the gap between the stated needs and how the buyer attempts to meet these needs.
4. Active listening is an important part of your needs analysis. You demonstrate your active listening skills as you patiently study and process the buyer's needs, wants, and fears. This enables you to formulate a strategy for meeting these needs.

CHAPTER 19

THE PRESENTATION STAGE

OK, LET'S REVIEW. You know how to open the sales call, and you've asked questions and listened patiently during the needs analysis stage. Now you take the next natural step on the value-added sales call as you enter the presentation stage.

It's time for you to tell your story relative to the buyer's needs. If buying and selling is an information exchange, the presentation stage is your opportunity to give enough relevant information about your solution so that the buyer is more willing to buy than you are to sell. The ability to persuade is an important skill for value-added salespeople. You must be able to present a compelling reason for the buyer to choose your alternative.

This chapter is about building and presenting a compelling argument for your solution.

Specifically, here's what I cover:

- The rules of the presentation stage
- Your general overview statement
- The importance of your three-dimensional message
- How to sell to the buyer's style
- Engaging your buyer
- Developing strong proof sources

Rules of the Presentation Stage

The first rule is to sell to the level of decision maker you're addressing. (The three levels are outlined in Chapter 6.) If you're selling to a Level-I decision maker, discuss logistics: packaging, price, ordering, options, color, sizes, freight schedules, delivery information, lead times, terms, and the like.

If you're selling to a Level-II decision maker, home in on usage: ease of use, training, technical support, safety, quality, convenience, compliance with specifications, and so forth. Users want you to make their jobs easier. Technical types want lots of data. Compliance types want no surprises and tighter specs.

If you're selling to a Level-III decision maker, a high-level employee, concentrate on results: increased profitability, greater performance, higher productivity, competitive gain, and similar goals.

Second, sell what's relevant. If the buyer spent a lot of time in the needs analysis discussing quality problems, present your quality as the solution to the problems. If a customer has delivery problems, describe how your delivery will meet these needs. If the buyer tells you that product availability is paramount, emphasize your product availability and inventory policy.

Salespeople have standard ways to present their products and to discuss their company—this is their pitch. Value-added salespeople modify their presentations depending on what they discover in the needs analysis. You can prepare a message in advance based on what you know about the customer and be prepared to be flexible in the way you present it. Planned does not mean canned.

Third, determine how long your presentation should be. Settling on the appropriate duration is tricky. It should be long enough to convince but short enough to hold the buyer's interest. The formula is similar to that of a good sermon: it should have a strong beginning and a powerful closing, and the shorter the distance between the two, the better. A priest in the church I attend delivers a great five-minute sermon. The problem is that he talks for twenty minutes! A guy in the oil business characterized this best when he said, "If you don't strike oil soon, quit boring."

General Overview Statement

It's important to have a powerful transition statement from the needs analysis to the presentation stage. This general overview statement answers these four questions in one hundred words or fewer:

- Who are we?
- What do we do?
- To whom do we sell?
- What makes us unique?

For example, "Mr. Buyer, Gemini Equipment Company is a forty-year-old supplier of specialty industrial gauges for chemical manufacturers. Our customer base ranges from small to large production facilities. What makes us unique is our lightening-quick turnaround time on special requests. We build to suit your needs."

This forty-seven-word overview gives you the opportunity to transition into the more detailed presentation of the features and benefits of your total solution. The general overview statement is also an effective statement to use when you're introducing your company to your buyer on the phone or during the opening stage of the presentation.

Keep it brief so that the buyer doesn't ask questions at this point. You want to maintain control of the conversation and direct it to relevant topics that underscore your value-added solutions.

Sell All Three Dimensions of Value

Don't you wish you had a dollar for every time I've discussed the three dimensions of value: your product, your company, and Brand-You (the value you bring to the table)? This deliberate redundancy serves a purpose: overlearning. I want you to remember this concept. Use Reilly's Rule of Threes: Give your buyer three relevant benefits in each of the three dimensions of value.

Make sure you sell relevant features and benefits of your product. One problem salespeople have when discussing their products or services is that they use claims, not features and benefits. For example, "We're the biggest and the best!" Says who? You've made a claim. It's your opinion. Claims pump you up. They're fun. They're exciting. They build your enthusiasm and allow you to express your passion. Be prepared, however, to back up your claims.

Unlike claims, features are specific. Features are facts that describe. They include physical aspects: the size, color, weight, and other specifics. They also include operational or functional elements: the number of revolutions per minute, the speed of a computer, a description of how something works, and so on.

A second problem salespeople have when discussing their offerings is that they recite a litany of features without extending these features into benefits. Features answer the question "What is it?" Benefits answer the question "Why is that important?"

Benefits are *why* the buyer chooses your alternative. Collectively, benefits answer the question that all buyers ask, "What's in it for me?"

To determine the benefit of a specific feature, ask yourself, "So what?" "Why is that important?" or "What does that mean to the buyer?" The answers to these questions yield the benefit.

Link your feature-benefit statements with connectors such as "this means," "this assures you that," "why that's important," and "what this gives you." In this way, you make the feature-connector-benefit statement conversational, natural, and relevant.

The second dimension of value is your company and its depth of resources. Explain your company's value-added services. Discuss your company's commitment to the value-added philosophy. Present your qualitative and quantitative value added. Elaborate on the resources available from your company to the customer. Position your company as *the* value-added supplier.

The third dimension of value is Brand-You. It's what you personally do for the customer. In Chapter 3, I explained the Value-Added Selling process and how your role evolves as the sale progresses. Detail for your customer how you deliver value at every step along this path. Remember, the same product from the same company from two different salespeople represents two different solutions. Your commitment and knowledge are essential benefits to the customer, and you must let customers know how valuable you are to them.

Sell to Your Buyer's Style

Some buyers move quickly and intuitively, while others move slowly and methodically. Some buyers are more concerned with people issues, while others are more task oriented. Buyers' priority and pace make up their style. Your mirroring the buyer's priority and pace is called *pacing your buyer.*

Pacing is important throughout the entire sales call. You took your lead from the buyer in the opening stage and asked questions in a way that made the buyer feel comfortable.

In your presentation stage, you must present your solution at a pace that mirrors the buyer's pace. Your features and benefits should reflect the buyer's priority: Is it task or people?

For task-oriented buyers, ask yourself how your product or service enhances or improves any of the following measures:

- Profitability or cash flow
- Task performance
- Market image
- Credibility
- Productivity
- Operational efficiency
- Product quality
- Competitive advantage
- Lead time

Again, for task-oriented buyers, ask yourself how your product or service helps reduce, eliminate, avoid, or alleviate any of the following problem areas:

- Waste
- Rejection rates
- Mistakes/errors
- Inefficiency
- Downtime
- Quality glitches
- Back orders
- Profit piranhas

For people-oriented buyers, ask how your product or service enhances or improves any of the following priority areas:

- Comfort in use
- User-friendliness
- Ordering convenience
- Employee morale
- Safety
- Employee relations
- Employee benefits
- Service
- Training
- Follow-up support

Another question to ask yourself for people-oriented buyers is how your product or service reduces, eliminates, avoids, or alleviates any of the following detractors:

- Risk
- Internal conflicts
- Employee stress
- Employee turnover/absenteeism
- Job-related hazards
- Morale problems

Presenting your solution in a way that your customer wants to buy is customer-oriented selling. This is the customer-value focus applied to a sales call.

Engage Your Buyer

In the needs analysis stage, your buyer played an active role in the process by being involved in answering your questions. This feedback helped you forge a solution that paralleled his or her needs. In the presentation stage, you do more talking, which means the buyer will do more listening. Even though effective listening requires the buyer to be active in the process, there is a danger that the buyer will assume a passive role here. Your job is to keep the buyer actively engaged during your presentation.

- ***Ask involvement questions.*** Draw the buyer into the conversation. Seek input on your discussion points. Ask these types of questions to engage the buyer: "Is this what you had in mind?" "Will this meet your needs?" and "Are these the results you had in mind?" You can open the conversation by asking, "How do you see this affecting your operation?"

  The added benefit of these opinion-seeking questions is that they are also trial closes. The responses you receive are an accurate indication of the buyers' interest in moving forward. Several positive comments signal that it's time to ask for a commitment.
- ***Project buyer ownership.*** Use possessive words and assumptive statements that imply that the buyer has already purchased your product or service. For example, "One of the benefits *you'll* enjoy with *your* new computer is the data transfer speed. It will trim *your* online time by half."

  This projected-ownership statement, laced with possessive words and assumptive statements, puts the buyer in the frame of mind of already having purchased your product or service and begun to enjoy its benefits. Some buyers need this type of help to visualize ownership.
- ***Use "we," not "me."*** Using the pronoun *we* draws the buyer into the presentation because it suggests teamwork and partnership. You and the buyer are working jointly to solve problems.
- ***Involve the buyer.*** Have the buyer do something. Some buyers are visual processors. Others, however, are tactile processors; they learn better by hands-on involvement. The power of hands-on product or service demonstrations is that they engage buyers actively in the process: the buyer does something. Being involved makes it easier for the buyer to appreciate the value of your offering.
- ***Give the buyer materials for selling internally.*** Enlist the buyer in your army of supporters who will help you fight your battle inside the company. The more that buyers promote your cause, the more

committed they become. Because they know the ins and outs of their company's politics, they weave through that maze more quickly than you can.

Use Proof Sources

- ***Support your case with credible sources.*** You reassure buyers when you demonstrate that others feel positively about your solution and are willing to go on record to prove it. Use testimonial letters and direct quotes. If your company has conducted customer satisfaction surveys, use the survey data to prove your point.
- ***Third-party endorsements are impressive.*** Endorsements speak favorably to buyers because the person giving the endorsement feels your product is a good buy. These include testimonials from trade magazines, Underwriter's Labs, *Consumer Reports*, and other well-known sources.
- ***Warranties and guarantees offer a special kind of reassurance.*** Your warranties and guarantees signal to the buyer that you will stand behind your product or service. If you use them as part of your sales approach, stress their positive aspects, not the remedies. Everyone has seen the retailers' ads that promote money-back guarantees. These ads stress the remedy for being dissatisfied. Instead, emphasize the positive, not the negative. Guarantee the buyer's satisfaction: "The benefit of our guarantee is that we work with you until you are *completely satisfied* with our solution." *Complete* buyer satisfaction is a powerful guarantee and an effective way to prove your worth to the buyer. Buyers want their money's worth, not their money back.

VALUE-ADDED SELLING REVIEW AND ACTION POINTS

1. Buying and selling is an information exchange. In the needs analysis, you listened to the buyer's needs; in the presentation stage, you discuss your solution to these needs. Your

presentation stage should be long enough to convince the buyer, yet short enough to hold his or her interest.

2. Buyers move at different paces and have different priorities. Some buyers advance through the decision process quickly, while others move with trepidation. Some buyers are focused on task issues, while others concern themselves with people issues. Tailor your sales approach to mirror the buyer's style.
3. Draw buyers into your presentation stage with the various involvement strategies listed in this chapter. Buyers become more passive as sellers begin their presentations. You want the buyer to be actively engaged in the buying process.

CHAPTER 20

THE COMMITMENT STAGE (AKA CLOSING)

You've opened the value-added sales call, asked questions in the needs analysis, and presented your solution. Now you're ready for the commitment stage of the sale—the point at which you achieve your call objective. Some people call it the action step, the close, or the logical conclusion to a series of events. It generally involves detail work to finalize your arrangements. Commitment accomplishes your goal.

Some salespeople believe that gaining buyer commitment is anticlimactic, because they anticipated fireworks that didn't go off. It was something less than amazing, because there was no magic in it for them. Indeed, that's the way selling should be. There are no good closers, just good salespeople.

If you've failed to do an adequate job of analyzing the buyer's needs and tailoring your presentation to these needs, it's difficult to resurrect interest during the commitment stage. If you rely heavily on closing techniques to get the business, you offend buyers at the worst possible moment—when you're asking them for money.

This chapter is about gaining buyer commitment and closing the sale. Specifically, here's what I do for you in these pages:

- Define closing and commitment
- Describe when to ask for the business
- Detail several ways to ask for a commitment

What Is Closing?

I prefer the word *commitment* to *closing*, because closing indicates finality. Commitment indicates a strong relationship and two-way accountability for a course of action. In Value-Added Selling, you don't close sales; you build commitment to a course of action that brings value to the customer and profit to the seller.

Commitment isn't an end point; it's the starting point for a course of action that solves a problem. Building commitment doesn't start at the end of the sale; it takes place throughout the presentation. As you study needs and propose alternative solutions, you're building commitment. You ask for commitments throughout the sales process. The point at which the buyer makes the final decision is where you ask for the business.

Commitment techniques describe how you ask the question that results in a buyer's agreement to purchase. While some people call these closing techniques, I prefer the term *commitment techniques*. Remember, commitment is something that you build throughout the presentation.

When to Ask for the Order

Asking for buyer action is a necessary step in the selling process. Nothing happens on your end until the buyer agrees to cut you a purchase order, write a check, or sign a contract. This is what you're paid to do—gain business. Never assume the buyer will come forward and volunteer to purchase without your asking. It may happen occasionally, but don't depend on it. The buyer may be unaware that the sale is approaching the moment of truth unless you say so. Ask for buyer commitment because without it, you're unable to provide the solution to the buyer's needs. Only commitment brings the solution that the buyer desires.

Asking for the order is a two-step process. The first step is asking an opinion-seeking question—sometimes called a trial close. You're asking for an opinion about your proposal. If the customer's response is positive, ask for a commitment. It's simple, it's practical, and it works! Remember: seek opinion, then commitment.

Knowing when to ask the opinion question is crucial. Timing is everything in sales: it's just as essential for you to know when to ask for the business as it is for you to know how to ask. This section highlights some techniques you can use to determine if the buyer's interest level is sufficient to pursue a commitment. You're looking for two types of buying signals: verbal and nonverbal.

Verbal buying signals are comments made by the buyer that indicate a strong interest in owning your product. The message could also be in how the buyer says something: a vocal change in inflection or the sudden display of emotion. Here are some sample phrasings that indicate a strong interest in buying:

- I think it may cost too much. (The buyer is really saying, "Sell me!")
- How soon can you deliver? (The voice connotes a sense of urgency.)
- Who pays the freight charges? (It's a matter of working out the details.)
- Is there a guarantee? ("Reassure me that I'm making a good decision.")
- Is there an installation charge? (You're working out the details.)
- I'd like to buy, but . . . (Whatever follows "but" is what you need to address.)

The buyer may also show interest verbally by repeating strong benefits you've mentioned and by asking more questions—especially questions of a technical nature. When the buyer uses possessive words such as *mine* and *our* to describe your product, it is sold. Real estate salespeople listen for prospective buyers to use the word *home* versus *house*. When you say "home" you've mentally bought it. Be attentive to such changes in verbal behavior. Listen for subtleties that indicate psychological ownership has taken place. Sometimes, it's the nuances that tell you when the time is right.

Nonverbal buying signals, the other side of the coin, are anything the buyer does to indicate a strong interest in your product. Be sensitive to nonverbal cues. Nonverbal indicators include stroking one's chin, leaning forward toward the seller, hand rubbing, caressing the product or the literature, smiling, giving a sigh of relief during the presentation, uncrossing of arms, and moving closer to the seller. All of these indicate that the buyer is seriously considering owning the product.

In Value-Added Selling, it's especially important to be sensitive to buying signals when you present nonprice factors. Watch for the prospect's interest level when you discuss freight, delivery, quality, technical support, or other such details. The buyer may *tell* you that he or she is not interested, but verify this attitude through the nonverbal signs. If the nonverbal signals indicate strong desire, go with them.

How to Gain Commitment

First, be alert to all of the verbal and nonverbal signals. Listen with your eyes and ears. Be prepared to seek commitment. Next, ask an opinion question to check the buyer's reaction to your ideas. Here are some sample opinion questions:

- What do you think?
- Is this what you had in mind?
- Will this do the trick for you?
- How do you feel about this?

These so-called trial closes are really the same involvement questions you asked during the presentation stage. Their answers tell you if it's time to ask for a commitment. Opinion questions (trial closes or involvement questions) precede commitment questions. If you get a positive response to the opinion question, ask for a commitment. The buyer is ready to purchase; go for it.

If you hear a pause or a hesitation from the buyer in response to your opinion question, pursue the reason. For example:

Salesperson: "How does this look to you?"

Buyer: "On the surface, it's OK."

Salesperson: "You sound hesitant?" (Pause for response.)

At this point, the buyer elaborates on the reason for the hesitation. Your job is to listen and deal with the resistance.

As you review the following commitment strategies, remember to always begin with an opinion question. Because you receive a positive response to your question, you feel confident asking for a commitment. Demonstrate this confidence in the action you ask the buyer to take.

- ***Assumptive technique.*** With this technique, take a matter-of-fact approach: assume the sale has taken place. Your assumption is implicit in the statement you make. You want to capitalize on the momentum you've established. Unless the buyer stops you, proceed because the sale has been made. For example: "If you feel this gives you the quality you need, let's schedule delivery for next Monday." Or: "Since this offers you the shipping flexibility you require, I can have this out here tomorrow afternoon if you'd like!"

  Each of the statements just cited seems like the natural conclusion to the events that preceded it. Further, each one refers to a benefit. Anytime you can include a benefit with your request for action, you reinforce the reason why the other person should purchase your solution. It reminds the buyer of the advantage of going with you—the benefits he or she receives.
- ***Summary technique.*** With this technique, you recap the major benefits you offer and follow this summary with the assumptive technique. Use this strategy to refocus a conversation that has gone astray in the presentation stage. For example: "Our next-day delivery reduces your lead time, and our product quality gives you the opportunity to be more competitive in your market. Let's schedule your first delivery for next week."
- ***Immediate advantage technique.*** There are two ways to use this technique: the right way and the wrong way. The wrong way is more appropriately called the "doomsday" technique. With the doomsday, you try to intimidate and browbeat the other person into buying. You warn the customer that something bad will happen if he or she doesn't act now. You threaten limited inventory, price increases, or any other potentially negative situation. Because of its effectiveness,

sales trainers have taught this strategy for years, but salespeople have abused it.

Consumers are desensitized to this approach and, in many cases, repelled by it. They feel backed into a corner to make a quick decision. For example: "If you don't give me an order right now for these goods, I can't guarantee you'll get them on time, because we have limited stock available."

The right way demonstrates a more positive approach: this is the "immediate advantage," in which you explain why it's advantageous for the buyer to press ahead and make a decision to go with you. You're still capitalizing on a sense of urgency, but you're doing it in a more positive way. For example: "The real advantage of your moving on this right now is that, because we currently have inventory, we'll be able to guarantee you the delivery you want when you want it, so that you can stay competitive in your market."

With this technique, you're stressing the advantage of moving ahead now as opposed to the disadvantage of waiting. It's a much more positive approach for your buyer than the wrong way—the doomsday.

- ***Alternate choice technique.*** With this commitment technique, you're asking the buyer to choose one of several options. Some people believe it's easier for buyers to select on a minor point (such as color or size) than to decide whether or not they're ready to buy. While I believe that if the prospect is ready to buy, he or she will buy regardless of how you ask, I include this technique as a convenience. Some salespeople have an easier time asking for the business with the alternate choice versus asking directly for a commitment. Here are some ways you can use this technique:
  - Which would you prefer, the blue or green unit?
  - Would you want to go with the 90-day or 180-day certificate of deposit?
  - Do we need a written purchase order, or is your oral commitment enough here?

Your strategy presents an alternative, an either/or selection. Be sure to present options with which you can live. You don't want to offer a choice of items that would cause you difficulty.

- ***Physical action technique.*** Some sales require the buyer to sign a contract, fill out an application, or complete a formalized purchase order. In these cases, handing the buyer a pen with the contract and asking for a signature is appropriate. Be careful with the wording you select. Try to avoid anything harsh that would turn the buyer off. For example, avoid this type of statement:
  - I'll need you to sign your life away here!
  - Put your John Hancock here, if you would!

  Even though you're presenting both of these statements in good fun, treating the business and commitment lightly may irritate the buyer. Try for something softer:
  - I'll need your OK for us to get the wheels turning on our end.
  - We'll need your approval right here to begin your service.

  Also, point out that it's a mutual commitment, because you've had to attach your signature to the document also, thus creating an atmosphere of teamwork and camaraderie.
- ***Concession technique.*** There are times in sales when the buyer asks you to concede on terms, shipping costs, FOB point, or the like. If the deal is good for you, give the request consideration. Pursue it before saying "No!" This is the concession technique, and here is how it sounds to your customer:

  "Mr. Prospect, I'm not sure we'll be able to give you the terms you're looking for, but I'm willing to go to my boss and run it by him. In order to do this, I'll need a firm commitment from you because he will ask me, 'Is this person shopping or buying?' If you give me a firm commitment based upon our meeting your demands, I'll pursue it. Please understand that I can't say yes. My boss will have to OK it."

  There are two major advantages to this technique. First, you're going to your boss with a firm commitment for an order. He or she can decide whether or not to write the business. Second, because the buyer has made a commitment, it's possible that, even if you're unable to agree to the concession, the buyer will go ahead and say, "You've got the business anyhow, but you owe me one!" It may be easier for the buyer to award you the business than to reopen negotiations with someone else.

- ***Direct technique.*** This technique is a straightforward request for action. There's no doubt what you want. You want the buyer to give you a commitment to act, and you make it plain because of your wording. For example:
  - I'll need your purchase order number to ship these goods!
  - Where would you like the material shipped?
  - Where would you like to go with this from here?
- ***Stall technique.*** When you sense that the buyer is hedging or stalling, dig deeper. Discover the real problem by smoking out any hint of resistance so that you can answer the buyer's concerns. The stall technique gives you a systematic way to persist. When you ask an opinion question and receive a dubious answer, try these questions:
  - You still sound hesitant . . . (Pause and let the buyer respond.)
  - What do you feel must happen on your end for you to go with us?
  - Do you see any reason at this point why you wouldn't go with us?
- ***Future-order technique.*** There are times when you sell the buyer on your product, but he or she has no immediate need: taking on additional inventory would not be a good business decision. You thus want a firm commitment for an order that will materialize in the future. While you may not be able to get an iron-clad commitment, any commitment at this point gives you a greater likelihood of getting future business.

  To your prospect, you say, "Mr. Buyer, since you like the quality of our product (or another nonprice benefit) and our delivery capabilities, can we depend on your commitment to give us a try the next time you order?"

  At this point, wait for the buyer to say yes. Ask a question that increases the buyer's feeling of accountability: "Would you mind if I followed up with you in a couple of weeks just to see how things are going?"

  Your second question alerts the buyer that you are going to ask about inventory again on your callback. Because he or she will face you again and knows it, you have a much better chance of securing a future order. The buyer feels more firmly committed, and for you, any commitment is better than no commitment at all. Your buyer won't want to refuse what he or she has already promised you. Most people like to keep their word.

- ***If/when Technique.*** Whether you're following up with a customer or just trying to firm up a commitment on your call, this technique works well. Similar to the other commitment techniques I discussed for reluctance situations, this technique helps you identify the likelihood of your doing business with this person.

  Here's what your words sound like with this technique: "Ms. Buyer, because we are interested in your business and would just like to know where we stand, is it a question of when you're going to order, or is it still a question of if you're going to order?"

  In this way, you can clarify whether or not the buyer has made a commitment. You're asking if the sale is just a question of time, yet you get one step closer to a firm commitment. If the sale is a matter of when and not if, determine your customer's timetable and find out what must happen from your customer's perspective for this sale to go through. Identify obstacles or potential barriers, and try to do something about them. If it's still a question of if, dig deeper to identify unresolved questions or doubts.

Value-Added Selling Review and Action Points

1. Closing is achieving your call objective. It's securing buyer commitment to the next logical step in the decision process, advancing the sale to its natural conclusion. Nothing happens until you ask.
2. Close when the buyer is ready to buy. He or she will send verbal or nonverbal signals indicating a desire to move forward. Ask two questions: an opinion-seeking question, sometimes called a trial close, and a commitment question, sometimes called a closing question.

The Value-Added Selling Format

These are the four steps you go through on each value-added sales call. You can also use this outline to plan your calls.

- *Opening Stage*
  - Introductions (and pleasantries)
  - State the purpose of your call
  - Ask permission to probe
- *Needs Analysis Stage*
  - Situational questions:
    General information
    Specific need
  - Competitive questions:
    How-met
    How-well
  - Projective questions:
    Ideal
    Impact
  - Summarize needs
- *Presentation Stage*
  - General overview statement
  - Present specific features and benefits for all three dimensions of value
  - Sell to the buyer's style
  - Ask involvement questions
  - Offer proof sources
- *Commitment Stage*
  - Opinion questions
  - Ask for a commitment to action

CHAPTER 21

HANDLING OBJECTIONS

REACTING TO OBJECTIONS means you wait for the objection to surface and then address it. This concept encompasses time, not assertiveness. Being responsive doesn't mean that you're surprised or bushwhacked; it means that you respond only after the objection has been raised. In most cases, you probably anticipated an objection and are prepared with a response.

That's what this chapter is all about, prepared spontaneity—being ready for an objection. Readying yourself means projecting yourself into the rejection situation so that you're primed for whatever comes your way. Preparation builds your self-confidence to face the objection and to be persistent without being a pest—tenacious in a nonthreatening manner. This chapter is about persistence in the face of resistance.

Specifically, here's what you receive from this chapter:

- Tips for handling objections
- A three-step communications model
- Ways to respond to price objections

Tips for Handling Objections

Before delving into the mechanics of handling an objection, it's important to understand a few basic concepts that can make your life easier in this resistance situation. Those fundamentals are embodied in the advice presented here.

- ***Divorce your ego from the sale.*** Remember that when the buyer rejects your product, it's not a direct assault on you. The rejection doesn't mean that you're a crummy person and the buyer wants nothing to do with you. For one reason or another, this buyer is not sold on your product. Don't get defensive, and don't argue. You can defend without being defensive. I don't know any salesperson who won a sale by winning an argument with the client, though I do know several salespeople who won the argument and lost the sale. Be tactful with your responses. Objections represent tenuous situations at best.
- ***Create an objections file.*** One way to be prepared for an objection is to have an objections file that contains potential responses to possible objections. Being prepared builds your self-confidence. Update your file regularly by adding new objections and responses. Review previously used responses and change the wording if appropriate. Why depend on your mind to store all this material? Make a commitment to yourself to create this file.
- ***Anticipate objections in a positive way.*** They will happen. Facing resistance is an occupational hazard, and there's no way to get around it. If you anticipate (not create) objections, you are able to maintain a more positive mental attitude, because these objections do not throw you off guard. You accept that they'll happen.
- ***Help the buyer save face.*** If the objection indicates that the buyer misunderstands what you've presented, give the buyer an opportunity to save face. You may even want to assume partial responsibility for the misunderstanding by saying, "Maybe I didn't explain this fully enough." or "What if we go over a couple of things again? I could have missed something." Exonerate the buyer and give him or her a chance to bow out of a situation gracefully. The buyer will reward your tact.
- ***Listen with all of your senses.*** Be totally perceptive. Listen for what's being said as well as what's not being said. How does the buyer express objections? What is the buyer's mood? How tentative is his or her concern? Try to fully understand the emotion as well as the facts.

- ***Be persistent.*** Many salespeople quit on the first "no"! Some quit on the second "no." If you persist until the third "no," you'll be with the top tier of salespeople who realize that perseverance is a virtue. The goal is to be persistent without being a pest. You can achieve this if you use the three-step communications model described in the next section.

Three-Step Communications Model

The dynamics of dealing with an objection are the same regardless of the nature of the objection. While you can use the model presented in this section for any objection you encounter, the major emphasis here is how to quell price objections. The process includes three steps: clarify, buffer, and answer.

Clarify

When you clarify an objection, you want the buyer to expound, elaborate, or discuss the concern more fully so that you can build your understanding of the objection as well as allow the speaker to ventilate emotion. If the buyer elaborates, it gives you time to think of a response, and the buyer may even talk his or her way out of an objection.

Clarifying generally involves one of two strategies. You can either ask an open-ended question about the objection or restate it in your own words, making the objection a question. For example:

Objection: "Your price is much higher than the competition!"
Open question: "When you say we're higher, could you be more specific?"
Restate: "Is it a question of our being justified in charging more than the competition?"

When clarifying a price objection, probe to discover the underlying motivation. Be sure that the buyer is making an apples-to-apples comparison. Is the comparison product exactly the same as yours?

Is the buyer concerned with the total cost of owning your product or just the acquisition cost? The cost to own includes operating costs, the amount of money you can save a buyer, the amount of money you can earn for the buyer, and the life cycle of the product.

Determine if price is the buyer's only consideration in purchasing your product. Check the buyer's expectations. Unrealistic objectives may be driving this price objection.

Another variable is the availability of funds. Your price may not be too high for the value you deliver; it's just too high for the budget this person has available. Your price is fine; the buyer's budget is too low.

Some buyers want a cheaper price in order to be more competitive in the marketplace in which they operate. They may think that the only way to compete is by offering their customers a lower price tag. You may be able to offer ideas on how to compete with nonprice value.

A final point of clarification is whether or not the person to whom you're selling actually has the requisite buying authority. Can this person say yes and no? Is this person the decision maker or an influencer?

Clarifying is digging deeper. It's probing to unearth any additional concerns. When you clarify, you want your counterpart to discuss objections openly.

Clarifying means that you're in the ask mode versus the tell mode. When most salespeople hear an objection, they go to the tell mode and try to overwhelm the customer with prepared rebuttals. This reaction is not as effective as going to the ask mode, which gives the customer an opportunity to expound.

Buffer

The second step in managing an objection is to buffer it. This means showing partial agreement, empathy, or understanding regarding the other person's concerns. In effect, you're saying to the buyer, "I'm on your side; I understand your concerns." Your empathy shifts psychological ownership of the objection. You're saying, "We're in this together." Here are some examples for buffering an objection: "I understand your position."; "I hear you."; "Yes, money is one concern."

Notice that I am not saying, "Don't buy, because our price is too high." Instead I'm saying, "Money is one concern, not the whole ball of wax—just one! There are other things to consider."

When you combine the clarifier and buffer, your dialogue flows smoothly. For example:

Objection: "You're charging more than I thought we'd have to pay!"
Clarify: "What did you anticipate paying for this?"
Buyer: "About 75 percent of what you're charging!"
Buffer: "I can see why you're concerned."

Here's an example of how to use the clarifier with the buffer in a nonprice objection:

Objection: "I don't like your delivery schedule!"
Clarify: "What is there about the schedule that you dislike?"
Buyer: "We need a twenty-four-hour delivery."
Buffer: "I understand. That is a legitimate concern."

One note of caution: Avoid the yes/but technique. When you use the word *but*, it negates anything preceding it. It's argumentative. Also avoid the words *however* and *although*; they're multisyllabic ways of saying "but." Review the following yes/but buffers, and consider how saying "but" negates the empathy.

- I understand your concerns, Ms. Prospect, but there is another way to view this!
- I hear you, but look at it my way.

Both are argumentative and telegraph that you're preparing to slam-dunk the person. You can always use *and* versus *but*. For example:

- I understand your concerns, Ms. Prospect, and there is another way we can approach this.
- I hear you, and let's examine another option.

The yes/and technique is much softer, and it allows you to assert your position in a nonargumentative manner. Everyone who attends my seminars tells me that this is the toughest habit to break. Don't despair—it's tough, *and* you can do it.

Answer

After you've clarified and buffered, answer the objection in one of four ways:

- ***Inform the buyer.*** State additional relevant features and benefits regarding your solution in order to either convince your buyer or correct a misunderstanding regarding your product, company, or service. In either case, your task is to provide additional information to establish that your solution is a good match for the buyer's needs.
- ***Review the buyer's needs.*** Buyers may object because they don't feel that they need what you sell. It makes sense at this juncture to review the buyer's needs and buying criteria. The review-needs strategy works well when the other person hesitates or stalls. When you review needs, ask buyers to reiterate what's important to them. Articulating one's own needs in this way increases the speaker's motivation to change.
- ***Use the alternate-advantage overload.*** If there's a particular feature that a buyer dislikes, overshadow it with features that he or she desires. Your objective is to demonstrate how the buyer is making a relatively small trade-off to get all of the other desired benefits. You in essence return to the presentation stage and embellish your description of these features, benefits, and value-added services to increase the buyer's desire enough to offset price.
- ***Reverse the objection.*** When you reverse an objection, you make it the reason to buy your product. For example: "Ms. Buyer, the fact that you are hesitating indicates to me that you want to make a good buying decision. If that's the case, that's exactly why I feel you need to go ahead with our product, since we've demonstrated its superiority relative to your needs." At this point, emphasize the specific features and benefits that are an advantage to the buyer.

Each of these four answer strategies requires you to retrace your steps to an earlier stage of the selling process. You'll either go back to the needs analysis to generate additional motivation or return to the presentation stage. If you view your answer strategy as reentry into a previous stage of the sale, the sales call flows smoothly. If you're unable to sell successfully on this call, your answer strategy may represent a follow-up call objective—the reason for your next sales call.

Price Objections

"Your price is too high!" These are the five most dreaded words for salespeople—the number one problem that haunts them. Price objections are a daily reality in sales. You hear lots of them. "There is hardly anything in this world that a man cannot make a little worse or sell a little cheaper, and the people who consider price only are this man's lawful prey," John Ruskin wrote more than one hundred years ago.

You are not the first generation of salespeople to deal with price objections, nor will you be the last. The fundamental reality of price objections is that buyers have a closer eye on what they're giving than on what they're getting. They're thinking more about the money leaving their company than the solution they're receiving from you.

When it comes to countering price objections, you want to have the optimal frame of mind. The advice in this section can help you gain a better psychological position for the negotiation.

One ploy is to slow down the process. Your two biggest enemies in dealing with price objections are time and emotion. Buyers know that if they push you on time, you will make an emotional decision that will benefit them. You need time and distance to make a good selling decision.

Another is to ask yourself: If your deal is that bad, why are you still in the game? This was an internal monitor I used as a salesman. When a customer told me about the great deal that the competition offered, my reaction was: Why didn't the customer jump on that great deal, versus telling me about it? For some reason, the deal stunk, and the buyer decided not to go for it. If that's the case with your buyer, why should you have to be cheaper?

In a similar vein, if your product is better than the competition, why should your price have to be lower than the competition? Why shouldn't your quality and service be the standard, versus the competitor's price? Remember, there's no such thing as a free lunch. If you offer more, you're completely justified in charging more.

Be better prepared to deal with the price objection than the buyer is to object. Be proactive. Anticipate objections positively, knowing that you may hear them. Plan accordingly. Whoever is better prepared, you or the buyer, emerges victorious in a negotiation.

Whenever you're confronted with a price objection, go to the ask mode versus the tell mode. Determine what the customer is really saying. Probe for the motive behind the objection. For example, you could ask the buyer these questions: "When you say we're higher, could you be more specific, please?"; "How is our price higher? Please elaborate for me."; "What did you anticipate the price to be?"; "Is price your only reason for hesitating?"; "When you say our price is higher, what are you comparing it to?; "Are you talking about the purchase price or the ownership cost?"

The purpose of your clarifying the price objection is to understand exactly what the buyer is saying. Before you can respond to an objection, you must understand the buyer's point of view. Is this a real or contrived objection?

Once you understand exactly what the buyer is saying, you can respond to the price objection in one of the seven ways outlined here.

Discount

Suggesting that you discount may sound odd in a book that teaches you how to sell value added, but I'm a realist. I know there are times when you will discount. The key to your discounting is that it must be strategic, not accidental.

Discount when it makes sense. If it fits your overall strategic plan and does not confuse the market, discounting could make sense. Discounting is a management and marketing decision, not a salesperson decision. Before you offer customer discounts, check with your management or marketing department to determine if the discount makes sense. When discounting, maintain your credibility by cutting something from your package to justify lowering your price.

Also, never give a discount without a firm commitment to buy. Otherwise, your buyer will shop your price with the competition. If the buyer is reluctant to give you this commitment, you didn't have the order to begin with. Never leave your discounts open-ended. Put a time limit on them so the buyer knows this will not be an ongoing situation. Convey the message that it's a special pricing action for a specific transaction.

Change the Package

Either add value to the package (bundling) or remove something from the package (unbundling). Change the package in some fashion so that either the buyer feels better about the higher price or you feel better about lowering your price to meet the price objection. Look for ways to add value or subtract value from your package.

Ask Thought-Provoking Questions

Ask questions that cause the buyer to rethink his or her position. For example: "Why do you think the competition is cheaper? They obviously know something about their product that we don't know."; "Why do you think they're discounting?"; "Considering your objectives, is a price-only buying decision the safest decision you can make?"; "Have you given any thought to what you may not get tomorrow that you are accustomed to getting today?" These questions may cause the buyer to second-guess the chosen strategy of going with a cheaper price.

Explain Your Value Added

Reiterate the value added that your company brings to the table. Acknowledge the higher price, and use it as a springboard to repeat your value-added benefits. For example, "Yes, our price is higher, and the reason we're higher in price is that we are higher in every other critical area as well. You can't be high in those areas and low in price. It doesn't work that way in business." Explaining your value added is an educational process: you want buyers to realize that paying more means they will receive more benefits with your product. This is a great time to review your VIP list with your buyer. (See Chapter 4.) "These are all the reasons why I believe we are the right choice for your company."

Argue Your Case from the Buyer's Perspective

Use the reversal. If your back-end value is greater than the competition's, this is the ideal technique to use. For example, "Ms. Buyer, if money is your real concern, that's exactly why you need to give our solution another look. When you look at our total value, you'll find that the cost to own our product is considerably lower than the competition. And if that's the case, that's exactly why you should purchase our offering today." By using the buyer's argument to justify your position, you turned a price objection into a money justification.

Reassure the Buyer

Buyers need assurance from you that paying more is a good idea. You can transmit this assurance in a number of ways. Some salespeople offer a personal guarantee. This makes great sense when the buyer knows that you plan to be in your territory for some time and you will have to either deliver on your promises or suffer the consequences. Referring to the warranty or guarantee that your company offers is another way to reassure the buyer. Remember, however, that anytime you stress your guarantee or product warranties, you want to promise complete buyer satisfaction, not just remedial action for the problem.

Deal with Them Later

There are times when buyers simply want to think aloud. A buyer may raise a price reservation early in the conversation but really not expect you to do anything about it. In this circumstance, you're better off not to acknowledge it one way or the other. If it surfaces again later in the sales call, you will know it was a legitimate objection. Otherwise, it could be something as simple as the person's thinking aloud.

Salespeople live with price objections daily. If you want more information on handling price objections, refer to my book *Crush Price Objections*. The entire focus of this book is price resistance: preparing to resolve price objections, avoiding price objections, and dealing with them as they surface.

Value-Added Selling Review and Action Points

1. Objections represent a break in your forward momentum. The objection could be a legitimate concern or hidden resistance masked by an excuse. Your challenge is to root out the reason behind the objection and resolve it to the buyer's satisfaction.
2. Prepare a list of rebuttals to the more common objections you may encounter. This simple preparation activity will boost your confidence and competence in dealing with sales resistance.
3. Price objections pose a special challenge for salespeople. Review the answer strategies in this chapter and select three ways to respond to price resistance, making the responses sound like you. The key to handling price objections effectively is to be better prepared to respond than the buyer is to give you an objection.

CHAPTER 22

POSTCALL ACTIVITIES

So FAR, YOU have planned and executed your value-added sales call. Now it's time to enter the third and final phase of the tactical side of Value-Added Selling: postcall analysis.

Specifically, here's what I share in this chapter:

- How to conduct an in-depth, postcall review
- Reilly's rules for follow-up

Postcall Review

What do you do when you finish your sales call? If you're like most other salespeople, you hop into your car and drive frantically to your next sales call. You may spend that travel time reflecting casually on your sales call or mentally preparing for the next call. If I were your sales coach, I would have another routine for you.

You and I would review your performance in the parking lot before we leave the customer's location. Why? Because everything is still clear in your mind. Writing your postcall analysis at the end of the day means you may forget something or run all of your calls together. A good sales coach will help you improve your performance immediately after the call.

Since I can't be with you on your sales calls, I'll give you some tips to help you develop your skills through a personal performance appraisal that you administer to and for yourself. Ask these questions about your performance before you leave the parking lot:

Was I focused? Did I stay on track? Did I wander all over the place with my presentation? Being focused is targeting the buyer's needs with relevant solutions, and resisting the temptation to meander by telling the buyer everything you know about your product and company.

Was it a good information exchange? Buying and selling is a dialogue, not a monologue. The buyer gives you information prompted by your questions, and you process that information to feed back a solution. The back-and-forth flow of your conversation produces a nonthreatening climate for the other person to tell you what's on his or her mind. The person can do that only when you're listening. Who did most of the talking on this call? Was there balanced participation?

How was the chemistry between the buyer and me? Did we click? Did we hit it off? Chemistry is one of the most important dynamics in selling. It's how well you interact with your buyer. Do you get along well with the other person? Even though chemistry is one of those intangible forces that operate beneath the surface, you can feel it in your gut and see it in the buyer's nonverbal signals. You know when you're in sync with the buyer.

Did I achieve my objectives? Chapter 16 stressed the importance of setting call objectives. Achieving these objectives moves the sale along the intended path and provides you with a yardstick to measure your success. This is especially true with your action objectives, what you wanted the buyer to do or say at the end of the call. Asking if you achieved your call objectives relates directly to the first question, regarding focus. How can you achieve your objectives without being focused? How focused can you be if you don't achieve your objectives?

As your personal sales coach, I would encourage you to ask yourself the preceding questions to help you understand the effectiveness of your efforts. Being busy is not enough. You must use your sales time productively.

Another coaching tip I would offer you is to schedule the next action step for this buyer before you leave the lot. This practice is a great timesaver, and few details slip through the cracks. Write the answer to the following question in your planner, input it into your PDA, or type it into your laptop: "Where do I go from here?" or "What's my next step?"

As you review your performance on this sales call, reflect on your successes as well as your failures. When I ask salespeople in my seminars how many of them perform an autopsy on a dead sale, more than half of them will admit to studying their failures. They ask, "What killed the sale?" Fewer than 10 percent ask the buyer this same question.

More astounding is that fewer than 5 percent will study their successes. Few salespeople will ask, "Why did we get the business in spite of our price, delivery, and specifications?" If you don't know what you're doing right when you're doing it right, how will you know what to do right when you're doing it wrong?

I've often heard salespeople and their managers say, "The best time to make a sale is right after you make one." They generally use passion, enthusiasm, or some other emotional energy as the reason. I agree with them, partially.

Yes, enthusiasm is contagious, and passion sells. But success cuts deeper than that. I've trained enough successes and failures in sales to formulate a theory: Everyone has a unique success profile and style that works just for him or her. I've met salespeople who were incredibly successful because they came from the service department and understood their business inside out. I've met salespeople who were successful because of their charisma; customers loved them. I've met salespeople who were successful because of their strategic thinking and planning abilities; they were master strategists. I've met other salespeople who possessed incredible product knowledge; customers felt compelled to do business with them.

Why are you successful when you're successful? Why do you make sales in spite of the obstacles you encounter? Study your successes. Learn from them. Feel the excitement, and leverage this passion and knowledge into greater successes. Nothing breeds success like success.

Reilly's Rules for Follow-Up

A basic principle of Value-Added Selling is follow-up, follow-up, and follow-up. Buyers rate following up as one of the most important things a salesperson can do, yet it is one of the areas in which salespeople are weakest. This inverse relationship presents you with a golden opportunity. Follow up consistently, and you'll be ahead of the pack. These guidelines will help you improve at follow-up:

- ***Whatever time frame the buyer tells you, cut it in half.*** I have discovered that buyers often exaggerate how long it takes to make a good decision. The times that I waited the full duration, I discovered that they had already taken action with someone else. If they say, "Call back in four weeks," call back in two weeks.
- ***Always seek permission to follow up.*** Asking permission has several benefits. First, the buyer knows you will call again and feels obligated to give you a fair deal. At the same time, it demonstrates your willingness to serve even without business. In addition, when the buyer gives you permission to follow up, you feel less intrusive. You're not a pest. You've been told, "Sure, call me back if you like."
- ***Call back for a different reason.*** Tell the buyer you want to follow up to see if he or she has any questions—or whatever other reason you create.
- ***Call back when it's convenient for the other person.*** Find out the best time to call, and you'll feel even less intrusive. Combine this rule with the previous two to ask one question: "Mr. Buyer, because I am interested in your business, I'd like to follow up to see if you have any questions before making the final decision. When is it most convenient for me to call—early morning or late afternoon?" When the buyer answers, you have permission to follow up. You're not a pest; you're delivering a value-added service.

  If you sense that the buyer is becoming uneasy with your persistence, explain that the reason you are persistent is that you are interested in his or her business and want an opportunity to prove it, even when you haven't received any business yet. Tell the buyer your persistence is actually a benefit: if a problem surfaces after the sale, you'll be equally persistent in finding a solution.
- ***Establish how many unsuccessful callbacks you'll accept before calling it quits.*** Don't be a prisoner of hope. Effective salespeople know when to hold 'em and when to fold 'em. At some point, you must change your strategy for dealing with a buyer who continues to string you along. Leverage your sales time effectively.

- ***Always have a good reason to call.*** Make buyers feel that the time they have invested with you on this sales call is time well spent.
- ***Be innovative with your follow-up ideas.*** Send news articles of interest (especially about your company); send premium incentives or giveaway advertising items with your name on them; or do something thoughtful for your buyer's office or staff: for example, send flowers, bring doughnuts, or have a lunch catered.

Value-Added Selling Review and Action Points

1. Postcall review is integral to the tactical side of Value-Added Selling. In postcall review, you reflect on your performance and schedule your next action step.
2. Buyers rate follow-up as a top priority, but salespeople woefully underperform in this area. In fact, a lack of salesperson follow-through on promises is a major complaint by buyers. Seek buyer permission to follow up, and deliver on your promises.

PART IV

VALUE-ADDED SELLING—SPECIAL TOPICS

TO HELP YOU understand the flow of Value-Added Selling, Part I introduced you to the core value-added philosophy and presented you with supporting data to capture your buy-in. Part II described the Value-Added Selling Process™ and detailed the eleven strategies that value-added salespeople use. Part III was the tactical side of Value-Added Selling. Here, I taught you how to plan, execute, and evaluate your efforts. Part IV is real value added. The chapters in this final part deliver tangible value added for your sales efforts

Chapter 23, "Hi-Level Value-Added Selling," explains the benefits of calling on high-level decision makers and how to do it. Fewer than 10 percent of all salespeople call at this level. Your effectiveness in this skill area differentiates you from 90 percent of your peers.

In Chapter 24, I discuss the impact that technology is having on salespeople. Every generation of salespeople experiences a paradigm shift that significantly affects the sales profession. Technology has spawned many of these changes. Your view of technology, as friend or foe, determines whether you thrive or just survive during these times of great change.

In Chapter 25, I offer you guidelines for writing effective sales letters and give you twenty-two sample letters that reinforce Value-Added Selling activities. Value-added salespeople make it a habit to do what other salespeople can't or won't do. Value-added salespeople make habitual what others consider a hassle, and writing sales letters is one of these tasks. Selectively and strategically using sales letters as a complementary tool augments your sales efforts.

Chapter 26 is about your most precious resource, time. You do not manage time; you manage yourself within the constraints time gives you. In this chapter, you will learn two important things: how to set priorities and how to remain focused on them.

Chapter 27 is a summary of the ideas you've read about in Chapters 1–26: the value-added themes, preparation, strategies, and tactics. It's a blend of where you've been and where you're headed. It brings closure while challenging you to embrace and act on the Value-Added Selling philosophy.

CHAPTER 23

HI-LEVEL VALUE-ADDED SELLING

OVER THE YEARS, I've noticed that salespeople shy away from calling on high-level decision makers (HLDMs). Salespeople do well calling lower in the organization, but when it comes to calling on HLDMs, they struggle. Apparently, I'm not the only one who has noticed this gap. In separate studies conducted by two major corporations and two leading universities, researchers discovered that most salespeople lack the skills and the motivation to call effectively at higher levels in an account.

This chapter is about calling at the top levels in an account, on high-level decision makers (HLDMs).

Specifically, I have the following purposes:

- Define Hi-Level Value-Added Selling™
- Explain the importance of this skill
- Detail how you can become more proficient in this area

What Is Hi-Level Value-Added Selling™?

The subject of this discussion is calling at the highest levels in your account, targeting the high-level decision maker who can say yes to your idea. Many people in an organization can say no. Few can approve. Why would you ever take "no" from someone who cannot say "yes"?

Hi-Level Value-Added Selling is important for a number of reasons. First, most HLDMs get involved early in the decision process for budgeting purposes. The earlier that you engage HLDMs, the greater is your input on their budgets. Second, when you call high in an account, people at lower levels treat you better; the relationship between your company and the customer is forged by broader business issues; and the sales cycle is shortened. HLDMs are action oriented. Third, you have less competition at the top. Fewer than 10 percent of all salespeople call at this level. Finally, HLDMs do not give price objections. If they like the idea, they find the money. I can't remember the last price objection I received from an HLDM.

So, why don't salespeople call on these HLDMs? To find out, we surveyed hundreds of salespeople, gave them nine possible reasons from which to choose, and had them rank-order their responses. Here are the top four reasons they reported for failing to call at the top:

- They're intimidated by the HLDM.
- They fear offending a lower-level contact.
- They lack the skills to do so.
- They don't believe the HLDM will meet with them.

Which of these apply to you? What's holding you back from meeting with the HLDM?

Facts About HLDMs

The HLDM is the person who can approve your project in spite of your price. HLDMs create money. This is my simple definition. If they have this authority, they are HLDMs.

Certain myths surround HLDMs. For example: They're difficult to contact and meet. False. I've heard plenty of stories that involve some of the highest-placed shakers and movers in business meeting with salespeople because the salesperson had the courage to approach the HLDM. Another myth is that HLDMs are bigger than life, they eat their young, and they have either a Harvard M.B.A. or a Yale law degree. Wrong again. A particularly odious myth is that they despise salespeople. How wrong can you get? Who do you think sells their goods and services?

I sell mostly to HLDMs, and I've never seen a sign in any of their offices that says, "We shoot every third salesperson, and number two just left!"

Here's a reality check: HLDMs are not better than you. They get dressed the same way you get dressed every morning. Many of them come from sales. You do not get to the top of any organization by being aloof and distant from others. HLDMs will meet with you. I know. I meet with them. They do think differently from most other people, however, and I'll get to that.

To maximize your efforts, avoid these turnoffs or red flags for HLDMs:

- Excessive chitchat. An HLDM who wants to know about the weather will tune in the Weather Channel.
- Feature-benefit product presentations that inundate with facts and minutia
- Failure to do your homework, which means not being prepared for your meeting
- Not understanding their business or their industry
- Talking versus listening to them
- Obvious questions that are self-serving
- Closing too early—especially when they're not buying
- Deal mentalities—you're focused more on the transaction or order than on the partnership

Here are some personality traits of which you must be aware when dealing with HLDMs:

- They are more direct in their communications.
- They like control and power—you will see their egos.
- They are decisive and generally strong leaders.

- They will take calculated risks.
- Most are visionaries. They have a dream and will share it with you if you ask.
- They live their passion. They put everything into what they believe.
- Time is their most precious resource. They manage it ruthlessly.
- They are discerning; they quickly discard that which will not help them achieve their goals.

The thinking style of HLDMs is different from that of most other people. They have twenty-twenty vision. They see the world from 20,000 feet and look forward twenty years. These are big-picture types who are engaged with results, not processes. As conceptual thinkers, they cut through labels and surface distractions to uncover the dynamics of a situation. They analyze facts and data for practical solutions that have an impact on the bottom line.

HLDMs are well read and informed. They devour business journals, books, and newspapers, but number one on their reading list is trade journals.

You can reduce the distance between you and high-level decision makers in several ways. Study to build your knowledge base. Learn how to think and talk as HLDMs talk. Read what they read, and go where they go. Take charge of committees. Build your comfort level with this class by schmoozing internally with HLDMs in your own company and meeting HLDMs in existing accounts. Become an information conduit about your industry. HLDMs will seek you out if you become an industry expert. Use endorsements, testimonials, and referrals to open the doors for you.

The most effective way to arrange a meeting with HLDMs is through a referral from someone whom they respect—either internal or external. The next most effective way is to set up a meeting with your management and the customer's management team—the HLDMs. I call this the high-level schmooze. Two-thirds of HLDMs say they prefer this type of high-level management meeting. A high-end direct mail piece that transcends the boredom of most of today's direct mail may also open the door to the HLDM's office.

Calling on High-Level Decision Makers

Preparing to meet with an HLDM is the same as preparing to meet with any other customer. It's imperative that you show up ready for business. Asking the precall questions listed in Chapter 16 will help you direct your efforts to HLDM priorities.

Apply the following tips to make the most of your meetings with HLDMs:

- Minimize the small talk and icebreakers. These are busy people. Get to the point.
- Deliver high-end leave-behinds such as binders or portfolios.
- Use time efficiently. For HLDMs, time is a vital commodity.
- Ask them to share their vision and opinions.
- Demonstrate your competence at the outset. Share some knowledge with them.

The needs and concerns of HLDMs include industry trends, company direction and future, competitive challenges, outside pressures such as the government, profit piranhas, underutilized resources, customer and employee satisfaction, cost of doing business, shareholder value, and corporate image.

Business owners, one category of HLDM, want control and freedom as well as simple, practical, street-smart solutions that reflect their individual needs. They think about money in terms of cash flow. The reality of running a small business is making sure you have enough money coming in to balance the money going out.

Corporate HLDMs, on the other hand, do things that are career expedient. Career is their main priority. They seek widely accepted, results-oriented solutions that gain quick consensus throughout the organization. They want to spread the risk and the credit. For the corporate HLDM, winning means not losing.

Ask questions that draw out the needs and concerns of your HLDM:

- Where do you see your industry headed?
- What is your vision for your company?

- What are your long-range goals for your organization?
- Tell me about your company's greatest success.
- What profit piranhas chew away at your bottom line?
- How would you define a successful relationship with your suppliers?
- What are the mission-critical activities for achieving your goals?
- What type of immediate impact are you looking for?
- What long-range impact are you seeking?

When presenting to the HLDM, develop strong proof sources that support your position: testimonials from high-profile customers, articles from reputable publications, and solid third-party endorsements. Discuss strategic alliances, cost containment, value creation, competitive advantage, employee satisfaction, control, consensus, cash flow, and profitability. HLDMs want answers to questions in your presentation:

- How does your solution support the HLDM's vision?
- How does your solution contribute to the HLDM's critical success factors?
- How can you help the HLDM's company reach the next level desired?
- Where does your solution fit into the corporate strategy?
- How does your solution have a significant financial impact on the HLDM's business?

VALUE-ADDED SELLING REVIEW AND ACTION POINTS

1. When selling to HLDMs, stress partnership issues, not just products. They will buy your idea if they believe you understand their needs on all levels. You may want to schedule a high-level meeting with you, your boss, and the HLDM.
2. Remember, HLDMs are visionary. In your meeting, ask questions that draw out the HLDM's vision for his or her company and discuss ways in which your solution supports that vision.

CHAPTER 24

TECHNOLOGY: FRIEND OR FOE?

THE LABEL "technology-savvy salesperson" ought to be redundant, but it's not. I'm still baffled by the large number of salespeople who do not use technology to their full advantage.

Whether you're a technophile or technophobe, this chapter is for you. It shows you how technology as a whole, not just SFA (sales force automation), augments and enhances the Value-Added Selling experience. Technology is much too broad a term and paradigm shift to be limited to contact management programs.

Since the mid-1980s, salespeople have seen major revolutions in technology that are at least as significant as the earlier transition from peddling one's goods by traveling aboard stagecoaches to flying coast-to-coast for a meeting and returning home in the same day.

Specifically, here's what I do in these sections:

- Examine the paradoxes of technology
- Argue the pros and cons
- Detail how technology fits in with Value-Added Selling

Technology Will Do What?

Technology carries its own special paradoxes and myths. It promised us a better, more efficient way to work and live. "It will simplify our lives," we were told at first. In reality, technology gave birth to a new form of type A behavior: techno-stress. We have learned how to do more and more in less and less time. We can now multitask—do several things simultaneously.

While sitting in rush-hour traffic, you can receive a fax, fax a reply over your cell phone, receive voice messages over your beeper, track your journey via the global positioning system, hear traffic reports on your radio, and listen to a book on your CD player.

Technology promised us a streamlined way to order goods via a World Wide Web. In reality, the lack of human contact has left many people craving the good old days when you could pick up a phone and talk to someone who would answer your questions in real time, not virtual time.

From these remarks, you might conclude that I despise technology. In fact, the opposite is true. I love technology. I embrace it as a tool to assist me. It serves me well. But therein lies the crucial difference. It serves me, not the other way around. It serves me, not enslaves me.

For example, when I started my speaking business in 1981, high tech in those days was three colors on a flip chart. We graduated to overheads with lettering machines. From there, we've grown to LCD projectors, video displays, and other presentation aids. These presentation aids make a mediocre presenter look better than he or she really is. That's a good thing—as long as the aids support the presentation. When the speaker supports the medium, it's all backward. Remember, technology must serve, not enslave.

The Pros and Cons of Technology

Technophobes are energized at this point by my commentary. I can hear them: "Right on, Brother Reilly." They contend that technology has made everything impersonal; that salespeople spend way too much time generating paperwork now that management has discovered the plethora of reports that are possible; that a lot of time is required to input information from sales calls into computers; that it slows the rep down; and that since fewer than 50 percent of all salespeople comply with management's request to use technology, it's really a waste.

The greatest of all antitechnology arguments is that technology will replace salespeople. Wrong! To paraphrase Mark Twain: The reports of the death of salespeople are greatly exaggerated. Selling is relationship management, and technology offers an enhanced way to manage the relationship. It complements the sales rep's efforts.

Humans are social creatures. We crave human interaction. Current scientific research demonstrates that the human brain works in a unique way when we are face-to-face with other people. Experimenting with various forms of technology, researchers have been unable to replicate the specific level of brain activity that occurs with human interaction. The telephone fell short. Online conversations fell short. Even video conferencing failed to produce the same level of brain activity as one-on-one contact. Humans are social creatures. Don't fight it.

Do you remember when telemarketing pundits foretold the death of outside calling in the early 1980s? It never happened, because the telephone is simply a complementary tool that enables salespeople to stay in touch with customers. The telephone could not replace face time.

Technology has its place in Value-Added Selling. Today's contact management programs enable salespeople to organize better than ever before. Fewer items slip through the cracks.

I have a major client who is a moving target. He globe-trots like a head of state. I can count on one hand the number of times he and I have been in the same time zone. Through E-mail and voice mail, we keep each other in the loop. When we need interactive feedback, we make time to track each other down. For the big discussions, I hop onto an airplane and visit with him face-to-face. Without technology, we would be strangers. With technology, we communicate.

You cannot minimize the impact technology is having on sales. To fight technology's impact makes the salmon's upstream swim look easy or the task of Sisyphus look like a walk in the park. Technology has affected salespeople and will continue to affect salespeople for the good, and maybe the bad, at times. You can either embrace it or get lost in the shuffle.

Technology enables you to be more accessible to everyone all the time. It gives you access to people you couldn't reach before. Your literature looks better. Technology enhances your presentations. You can give customers up-to-the-minute information regarding their orders because of it. You can file your expense reports more quickly and get paid faster. You can view your brother's newborn daughter the moment the hospital puts the picture on the Web. You can correspond with your peers in any part of the world. You can research products, competition, and customers electronically.

Failing to embrace technology in sales is professional suicide. Imagine complaining to a buyer about the impact technology has on your profession when this buyer places one-third of company orders over the Internet.

Customers will not stop using technology because you don't like it. They may use it even as a way to screen potential suppliers, which means that tech-savvy reps may enjoy competitive gain. The tech-sorry reps, on the other hand, may lose in the comparison.

Your company will not slow down to accommodate you because you reject technology. Customers may use it to weed out suppliers who add cost without value. The technology revolution is in full force. It's a tsunami, and you won't stop it. You won't even slow it down. Your resistance pales in comparison with its momentum. Get on board, or you'll get lost in its wake.

Here are some questions you must ask:

- What's reasonable when it comes to technology?
- How much technology helps, and when does it begin to hurt?
- What do I really need?
- Does it serve me, or do I serve it?
- Does it serve me, or does it enslave me?

Technology and Value-Added Selling

Technology has its place in Value-Added Selling. The Value-Added Selling process is conducive to opportunities management—the technophile's term for pipeline or territory management. In simpler days, salespeople managed territories and accounts. Today, they manage opportunities.

Opportunities management requires your sales process to contain several benchmark activities that follow the sales path from contact to contract. Managing opportunities is determining where you are with a prospect along this sales path.

For example, let's say your sales process follows this path: qualification of the account, demonstration of your product, formal proposal, commitment and confirmation, predelivery, usage, and growth. You have seven steps in your sales process. Managing opportunities is tracking how many prospects you have in each step and what you must do to advance the sale.

Technology automates this sales process as you use opportunities management software. It automatically tracks your programs with each opportunity, based on your data input. It may automatically generate sales letters, proposals, follow-up date reminders, and sales reports that you can E-mail to your boss.

In the Stone Age, salespeople had to maintain tickler files, chisel each sales letter out of stone, and send the information by snail mail. Today, they click and send.

Using opportunities management software requires you to first have an in-depth understanding of the activities that flow along your sales path. You can divide the concepts of focusing, persuading, serving, and after-marketing into activities that you plug into your opportunities manager.

Presentation software enables value-added salespeople to add sizzle to their presentations and proposals. Remember, however, that technology supports you. It's a sales aid. It does not replace the need for good presentation skills. It enhances and complements—it's no substitute.

I've seen good examples of how salespeople have logged on to a customer's website and downloaded graphics to integrate into their proposals and presentations. This degree of customization was difficult to achieve in the past. Add to this effort an inexpensive color printer and, voilà, you have a professional look that will differentiate you from the competition.

Technology enables you to be accessible to your customer. Beepers, cell phones, and E-mail have revolutionized buyer-seller communications. Cell phones, E-mail, and videoconferencing will not replace face-to-face selling, but they augment it nicely.

Salespeople can now log on to the Internet and check inventory status or track orders for customers on the spot. In the good old days, such tracking might have involved several follow-up conversations. Today, salespeople can spot-check.

In addition, salespeople file call reports and expense reports electronically and get their reimbursements more quickly. They share information with their peers around the world. They research competitors and customers at home in the evening. They customize literature and send E-mail promos to hundreds of customers with the click of a mouse. They attend sales training sessions and college courses online. They find all of Tom Reilly's books at tomreillytraining.com and order them.

Technology has put professional selling on a path, and there is no turning back. However, there are some reasonable questions to ask yourself about technology and how much is right for you:

- What do we really need from technology in order to do a better job?
- At what point do we cross the line and overuse or misuse it?
- Does it really add value to our efforts?
- How much is too much?
- Just because we can do it, should we do it?

Value-Added Selling Review and Action Points

1. Technology promised a more efficient way to live and work. In what ways has technology made your life easier or more difficult as a salesperson?
2. These commonsense questions should guide your efforts when it comes to technology:
   - Does it serve me or enslave me?
   - Just because I can use technology, should I use technology?
   - Does technology add value to my efforts?
   - Does technology assist me in better serving my customers?

SALES LETTERS

IN A FAST-FOOD, instant-gratification, communicate-at-the-speed-of-sound world, the art of letter writing has taken a backseat to other communication channels. E-mail, voice mail, and fax machines have replaced this age-old, proven method of communicating.

This chapter outlines one of our oldest and most effective ways to communicate—the sales letter. Specifically, I do the following for you:

- Itemize the benefits of using sales letters
- Demonstrate how to organize your thoughts
- Offer writing, formatting, and editing tips
- Explain how to use sales letters as part of the persuasion process
- Equip you with twenty-two sample letters you can use for various selling objectives

Why Write and Send Sales Letters?

"Why write a letter when I can pick up the phone?" asks the young sales rep. Another sales rep challenges, "Why go through the expense of stationery and postage when it's more cost-effective to click the Send button on my computer?"

Our electronic world discourages the usage of sales letters, and salespeople have bought into the usual arguments such as these:

- It takes a lot of effort to write these letters.
- It's difficult to write these letters, and I'm no writer.
- I just don't understand the benefits.
- Customers don't read them.

As a confirmed sales letter enthusiast, I offer a differing viewpoint:

- Every sales letter you send is a customized brochure for the recipient.
- You can use sales letters to surround your customer with a message.
- Every letter received is another marketing exposure.
- Sales letters position you as a professional.
- They differentiate you, because few salespeople use them effectively.

Value-added salespeople make it a habit of taking those actions that other people think are a hassle. At every step along your sales path, you have a specific sales objective that you can support with a timely sales letter. Here's the reality of sales letters:

- Customers do read well-written, customized letters. I recently pulled more than 20 percent with a direct mail letter campaign by using a well-crafted sales letter.
- Letter writing does not need to be painful. That's the premise of this chapter. We're going to make it painless for you to use the sales letter.
- With help, everyone can write sales letters.

Organizing Your Thoughts

Good writing requires planning, and planning begins with an objective. Answering the questions in this section will help you become more focused in your letter writing.

- ***What do I want to accomplish with this letter?*** For example, do you want to get an appointment, create interest, offer an apology, reinforce your value added, summarize a meeting with your customer, or create pull for a new product?

- ***Who is my reader?*** Along with firm objectives, a clear view of your reader helps you construct a letter that the person will read and act upon. Your first step is to visualize the recipient in your mind. Then, answer these questions:
  - What is this person's education? Be cautious of the level at which you write. How technical can you get with this person?
  - What does the reader need? What would this type of reader typically look for in a solution? What types of forces drive these needs? Knowing the reader's needs helps you pinpoint benefits to emphasize in the letter. You customize your solution to the buyer's problems.
  - What does the reader want personally? Aside from business needs, does the reader have a personal interest in the decision? What represents a personal win for the reader?
  - What does the reader fear? Identify the elements you think your reader might want to avoid, such as complexity in ordering, too much effort to implement the solution, or excessive risk in the decision to buy.
  - What benefits does this reader want? Desired benefits vary from customer to customer. Understanding what buyers seek in a solution enables you to tailor your message. Be sensitive to the level at which this person works. Business owners want different benefits from those sought by a purchasing agent or a home owner.
  - What action do I want from the reader at the end of the letter? For example, do you want the reader to call you, place an order, agree to take your phone call, request a sample?
  - What emotion do I want the reader to feel: excitement, curiosity, compassion, satisfaction, pride?

The more clearly you understand your objectives, the more practical value your letters will have. Well-written letters begin with a singleness of purpose that comes from your objective. A clear understanding of your objectives coupled with your insight into the buyer's world paves the way for an effective sales letter. A few minutes invested in preparation, asking and answering the foregoing questions, will pay huge dividends in results.

Formatting Tips

When setting up the document, use a standard format for business letters.

Use a formal date style. Always include a social or professional title (Mr., Ms., Dr.) in the first line of the inside address. The second line of the inside address is the reader's title. The third line is the company name. The fourth line is the street address or P.O. box number. The fifth line is city, state, and zip code.

The salutation may vary depending on whether the letter is going to a stranger or to someone you know. First names are fine if you know the person and commonly address each other by first names. The same applies to nicknames.

Keep your sentences and paragraphs reasonably short. Lengthy paragraphs lack eye appeal. Use adequate spacing and fonts to make the letter more readable. Support your claims with facts and proof sources.

Use an appropriate complimentary close to end the letter: "Your friend," "With warmest regards," "Sincerely," or a similar expression. In a persuasion letter, always add a postscript (P.S.) to reinforce the key concept. Research indicates that the P.S. is the most-read portion of the sales letter. I don't know why, or even care why. I use it and can confirm its effectiveness.

You can increase the probability that the reader will open your sales letter by doing the following:

- Use a nonbulk postage stamp.
- Do not use address labels. Labels make the letter look like bulk mail.
- Type "Personal" or "Confidential" on the envelope.
- If appropriate, use a nickname for the recipient.

Writing Tips

These writing tips will help you design and create sales letters that have impact.

- ***Speak to the reader directly.*** Use the word *you* to personalize the communication. Write your letter as you would talk to the person. Your letters must sound like you. One way to check on yourself is to read your words aloud. Your writing style should reflect your speaking style.
- ***Use the KISS principle—Keep It Simple, Salesperson!*** Choose your words carefully. A one-syllable word with punch beats the heck out of a four-syllable word that the reader doesn't understand. Impress the reader with your ability to get to the point, not with your vocabulary. Use concrete and specific language.
- ***Less is more—get right to the point.*** Leave lots of white space for legibility. You're competing for someone's most precious resource: time. Emphasize key words or thoughts with bold letters or underlines. Bullets are acceptable.
- ***Write with clarity.*** Avoid wordiness that attempts to make you sound intelligent; it does the opposite.

Use	**Avoid**
Now	At this time
No	Responded in the negative
We believe	It is our opinion
Many	A substantial number of

- ***Develop a positive attitude.*** Keep the tone of your letters positive and nondefensive. When correcting situations, fix the problem, not the blame. When handling problems, explain without excusing. Accept responsibility for solving the problem.

I use this personal checklist to keep my writing on track:

- Don't never use no double negatives.
- Never use a preposition to end a sentence with.
- The passive voice should be avoided.
- Use action words that leap off the page and grab the reader.
- Forget excessive punctuation. You know, the kind that often confuses; and that may even distract you, the reader, away from the main thought . . . As the writer: It's difficult, at best, to edit—if at all.

- Nouns and verbs are worth more than a million weak adjectives or flowery adverbs.
- Edet, eddit, edit.
- Avoid too-long sentences, as they tend to confuse the reader while diluting your message and will decrease the probability of the reader's taking the action that you planned for in your preparation stage before you sent the letter and you were still in the idea phase.

If you want to go that extra step in writing, use specific words and phrases to customize letters. You must know the reader well to choose which group of words to use. For example, hard-driving, determined, fast-paced, results-oriented customers respond favorably to the following words and phrases:

- Quick, fast, efficient
- Competitive advantage
- Gives you control
- Puts you in the driver's seat
- You'll want to experience this firsthand
- There's no apology for professionalism
- Maximizes your resources
- Productivity
- Energizes the troops
- Designed with your situation in mind

Expressive, emotional, fun-loving, and entertaining socializers relate well to the following usages:

- Fun, enjoyable, exciting
- Novel, new, leading-edge
- Great for your image
- Makes you look good
- Stylish, fashionable
- Creative
- Look who else is using it
- Makes you stand out

Laid-back, easygoing, and loyal types identify well with these words and phrases:

- Secure, stable, serene
- Safe decision to buy
- We're concerned about you
- Predictable
- Service-oriented
- Customer-driven
- We're here to support you
- Reliable
- Practical products for real problems
- Nothing fancy, but simple

Analytical types who are detail oriented, factual, and methodical—the thinkers—respond well to these words and phrases:

- Quality
- Guarantee/warranty
- In-depth solution
- No surprises
- Field-tested and proven
- Right decision for your company
- Thorough in its approach
- Comprehensive solution
- State-of-the-art
- The industry standard

Editing

In retail, the three magic words are *location, location, and location*. In writing, it's *edit, edit, and edit*! Putting your thoughts on paper is easy. Editing is the real challenge. This challenge becomes manageable when you break the process down into steps:

- ***Step 1: Read for flow.*** Read your letter aloud to hear how it sounds. Does it flow? Does it make sense? Will the reader hear what you intended to say? Make sure you read the actual words on the page. Sometimes we add or change words unwittingly.
- ***Step 2: Check spelling and grammar.*** Today's word processing programs all have spell-checking capabilities. These tools are an easy and effective way to help ensure correct spelling. Many also have a grammar tool that suggests usage changes. Assure proper verb-noun agreement. Read word by word (some people read end to beginning) to identify words that need changing.
- ***Step 3: Get personal.*** Always verify the name, company, and address of the person to whom you're sending the letter. It's insulting to misspell the customer's name or to use an incorrect address. It also says something about your professionalism.
- ***Step 4: Double-check the numbers.*** If your letter contains product code numbers, invoice references, or pricing, check the numbers twice. Anything you put in writing leaves you exposed. Accuracy protects you.

Persuasion Letters

Some sales letters you write have a specific objective to persuade the reader to do something—to take a specific action. An understanding of how persuasion works will help you write convincing letters of action.

- ***Step 1: Get the reader's attention.*** Use a statement or question to grab the reader. For example: "Many of our existing customers tell us that their worst nightmare is not being able to get a product when they need it."; "Do your salespeople sell value or price?"; "It costs six times more to find new business than to keep your existing customer happy."
- ***Step 2: Refer to a need that you know will register with the reader.*** In Step 1, you're reminded through the examples that availability, selling price versus value, and customer retention are key issues for most

companies. If you position your attention getter as the lead paragraph, you can expand on it in the next paragraph to reinforce the need. In the sample letter that follows, you will see how this works.

- ***Step 3: Promise a benefit.*** Once the reader recognizes the need, you must offer a solution packed with relevant benefits. This—the solution—is the hope the reader searches for in the letter.
- ***Step 4: Issue a call to action.*** Ask for something. Invite your reader to do whatever you had planned when you asked yourself earlier: "What action do I want from the reader at the end of the letter?"

The following sample persuasion letter illustrates the four steps of persuasive writing.

Dear Prospect:

Did you know the most pressing problem facing American business is economic uncertainty?

Ninety-one percent of business owners report that their greatest fear is not being able to react quickly enough to rapid economic forces that would adversely impact their business. They said they wanted ideas on how to respond quickly.

The Mifflin Letter provides up-to-the-minute economic news and analysis. It offers the kind of forecasting you need to maintain your competitive edge. It's packed with valuable information to help you predict trends in your industry so that you can get a jump on your competition.

I'll contact you in a couple of days to see if you would be open to hearing more about this significant newsletter. Why not write down three questions you'll have for me when I call?

Sincerely,
Thomas P. Reilly

P.S. Do you know the three things to look for in your market that indicate trouble on the horizon?

The persuasion letter has such a specific objective that it merits separate treatment in this chapter. Other letters may have different objectives that require different formats. Samples of these appear in the following section. A follow-up letter after a sales call, for example, may have this format:

- Thanks for the opportunity to meet
- Brief recap of the meeting, reviewing the customer's needs
- Statement of commitment to helping the customer satisfy these needs
- Action steps if necessary

Sample Letter 4 illustrates these points.

Sample Sales Letters

This final section gives you a variety of sample letters to use in different selling situations. Feel free to copy them and change them any way you want. To find more sample letters, rummage through your customer files. Select six typical letters that you have sent customers in the past. These letters can serve as templates. You can use sales letters for a variety of sales objectives. In this section, the heading that precedes each letter indicates how the letter fits into the Value-Added Selling Process.

Sales Letter 1: Getting an Appointment

You want the reader to take your phone call to determine a meeting time and date. Note that this is the persuasion letter from the previous section.

Dear Prospect:

Did you know the most pressing problem facing American business is economic uncertainty?

Ninety-one percent of business owners report that their greatest fear is not being able to react quickly enough to rapid economic forces that would adversely impact their business. All said they wanted ideas on how to respond quickly.

The Mifflin Letter offers up-to-the-minute economic news and analysis. It offers the kind of forecasting you need to maintain your competitive edge. It's packed with valuable information to help you predict trends in your industry so that you can get a jump on your competition.

I'll contact you in a couple of days to see if you would be open to hearing more about this significant newsletter. Why not write down three questions you'll have for me when I call?

Sincerely,
Thomas P. Reilly

P.S. Do you know the three things to look for in your market that indicate trouble on the horizon?

Sales Letter 2: Appointment Confirmation

You have secured the appointment and want to confirm it, while positioning yourself as a professional. You may choose to enclose some materials for the prospect to study before your meeting.

Dear Prospect:

This will confirm our appointment on Friday, September 1, at 9:00 A.M. at your office. I'm excited about our meeting and confident that we will find some solutions to your selling problems.

In the meantime, I have enclosed some material for your perusal. I hope you will find it interesting. Unless I hear from you prior to the above date, I shall assume that our meeting is still scheduled.

Sincerely,
Thomas P. Reilly

P.S. What would it mean if we could increase your margins by 10 percent?

Sales Letter 3: Create Pull

You want to create pull for a product or service; for example, to generate customer inquiries. (This exact sales letter pulled a 25 percent return from our mailing list.)

Dear Friend:

Follow-up, follow-up, follow-up!

This is the answer to the question "How do I maximize my sales training?" Salespeople and managers alike want to know how to get more bang for their buck!

Ongoing growth and development is the answer. You must create a learning culture. My new book, *Selling Smart!*, can help you achieve that objective. It's jam-packed with hundreds of bite-sized pieces of information. It's the perfect complement to any sales library. Or stick it in your briefcase and carry it around for those traveling and waiting periods when you want to invest your time effectively.

Call today to order your copy of *Selling Smart!* 165-page paperback edition for only $9.95.

Sincerely,
Thomas P. Reilly

P.S. Ask about our sales managers' gift when ordering in quantity.

Sales Letter 4: Postcall Letter

Use this letter to summarize your meeting with prospects and to keep your name front and center.

Dear Prospect:

What a great meeting!

I'm glad we had an opportunity to meet today. The direction in which we're moving on this project is exciting.

We agreed to some action steps before our next meeting:

- [Detail]
- [Detail]
- [Detail]
- [Detail]

I'll follow up as we agreed.

Again, I'm really excited about our working on this project together.

Regards,
Thomas P. Reilly

P.S. [Insert P.S. here]

Sales Letter 5: Summary of Needs

After meeting with your prospect, send a letter to outline your understanding of his or her needs.

Dear Prospect:

I enjoyed meeting with you today and look forward to working together on this project. I'm confident that our solution will meet your needs and then some!

Just a few lines to briefly recap my understanding of your needs:

- [Need 1]
- [Need 2]
- [Need 3]
- [Need 4]

Again, I'm excited about moving forward on this and will follow up as we agreed.

Sincerely,
Thomas P. Reilly

P.S. What would it mean to your company if we could [insert relevant goal]?

Sales Letter 6: Proposal Letter

When you're unable to deliver a proposal in person, this type of letter serves as a cover piece.

Dear Prospect:

Thank you for the opportunity to offer our plan for meeting your needs. I'm excited about the possibilities.

I've begun the proposal with a summary of your needs to ensure that our solution is built to your requirements.

Our customized approach to your needs reflects the value-added philosophy upon which we've built our reputation.

I plan to contact you shortly to discuss how our solution will meet your needs.

Sincerely,
Thomas P. Reilly

P.S. I know that timing is critical to your success.

Sales Letter 7: Letter of Commitment

Use this as one of the final pages in your proposal to reinforce the concept that you represent a value-added resource to the customer.

Dear Customer:

When you make a decision to invest in our total solution, part of that package is me. This is what I pledge to do for you as your sales representative:

I will provide full accessibility. Here are three ways for you to contact me. [Insert business phone, home phone, cell phone, E-mail, secretary's phone, etc., as appropriate.]

Systematic follow-up: 30-60-90-day immediate follow-up, with quarterly meetings thereafter.

Ongoing ideas—part of my pledge to bring you new ideas on a regular basis to improve our solutions.

Quick response to your requests.

I take my job as a professional seriously. I hope you will too. It is a pleasure to serve you.

Sincerely,
Thomas P. Reilly

P.S. [Insert P.S. here]

Sales Letter 8: Positioning Letter (Company)

Use this letter when you want to position your company in the customer's mind.

Dear Customer:

More great news from our company!

As you know, value added is a big part of our company's culture. And we love to talk about the new things we bring to the table.

We've recently launched this new value-added service as part of our commitment to excellence.

[Detail the service]

I guess you can tell we're so proud that we're about to burst. I'll follow up with you shortly to discuss this idea with you personally.

Best wishes,
Thomas P. Reilly

P.S. How will this value-added service benefit your company?

Sales Letter 9: Positioning Letter (Personal)

Use this letter when you want to position yourself as a value-added sales rep.

Dear Customer:

Just a brief note to bring you up-to-date on something of which I'm proud.

[Detail something about you personally]

I felt this would be something that you would want to hear. I guess you can tell it's important to me.

Thanks for your time and the opportunity to serve your company.

Sincerely,
Thomas P. Reilly

P.S. [Tie something into the customer here]

Sales Letter10: New Product/Service Announcement

This letter is designed for situations in which you want to introduce your customers to a new product or service.

Dear Customer:

We're thrilled, and we believe you will be too!

Because many of our customers have asked for a quicker way to handle their transactions, we have implemented a new order-entry system.

Our new EDI ordering system will save you $2,000 this year in transaction costs associated with purchasing. Additionally, we'll cut your lead time in half!

I'm sure you're as excited as we are about this value-added service. I'll call you shortly to arrange for an appointment to meet and discuss this.

Best regards,
Thomas P. Reilly

P.S. How will you use that $2,000 savings?

Sales Letter 11: Pressure Point Letter

This letter is used to recap your meeting with a customer and to list the appropriate buyer pressure points to deflect price objections.

Dear Customer:

I enjoyed our meeting today and look forward to working with you on your new program. I thought I'd take a few lines just to briefly recap our meeting today:

I know that timing is critical on this project, and I'm excited about our opportunity to meet your time lines. I was sorry to hear that you've been disappointed with alternatives you've used in the past.

It's great to hear how well your business is going right now. I know it's one of the reasons you want to move forward on this program.

It's great to hear that your folks enjoy working with our company.

As we agreed, I'll follow up with you next week to determine the next step in this process. Once again, it will be a pleasure to serve you in the future, just as it was in the past.

Sincerely,
Thomas P. Reilly

P.S. Our goal is to give you the support you need to achieve your goals.

Sales Letter 12: Gracious in Defeat

When you lose a sale and want to remain gracious in defeat, send this letter to demonstrate your professionalism.

Dear Prospective Client:

I've enjoyed working with you on this project. I know that you labored over this decision and are choosing the option that you feel is right for your company. I respect that.

I felt that the chemistry between us was strong and that you liked many of the things we brought to the table. Therefore, I'm optimistic. I'm sure there will be opportunities for us to work together in the future.

I wish you great success on this project and look forward to serving you again.

Sincerely,
Thomas P. Reilly

P.S. I'm here if you need support.

Sales Letter 13: Thanks for the Business

It's appropriate to thank your customers for their business. This letter praises the customer's decision and demonstrates your appreciation.

Dear Customer:

Congratulations on your decision to use our value-added solution, and thank you for the opportunity to serve.

We're excited about our working with your company to help achieve your objectives. We're confident that our value-added solution will meet your needs—and then some!

I plan to follow up as we agreed.

Sincerely,
Thomas P. Reilly

P.S. We know that you have high expectations for our service, and that's how we would like to be judged!

Sales Letter 14: Stay in Touch

When you just want to say "Hi" and stay in touch with your customer, this letter will serve you well.

Dear Customer:

Like the Willie Nelson song, "You are always on my mind . . ."

It's been a while since we've talked, and I wanted to touch base to bring you up-to-date on some things happening with us.

[Update information]

It's exciting for us, and I wanted to share this with you. I look forward to our next meeting.

Warmest regards,
Thomas P. Reilly

P.S. Sometimes you feel so good about what you do, you've just gotta tell someone.

Sales Letter 15: Customer Satisfaction

When you want to determine how customers rate your performance or that of your company, this letter can accompany a survey or questionnaire.

Dear Customer:

How are we doing?

In our early discussions I promised that follow-up was a big part of our value-added service.

The enclosed questionnaire is one way we solicit feedback from you on how we're doing. We use this information to grow. Please be candid.

If you would like to discuss this evaluation with me personally, please call me at your convenience.

Thanks for your input.

Sincerely,
Thomas P. Reilly

P.S. When we stop growing, we're going nowhere fast!

Sales Letter 16: Price Objections

When the customer has objected to your price and you want the last word, this letter presents your argument.

Dear Customer/Prospect:

Is price the safest decision you can make?

I left our meeting today concerned about the decision facing you. I know you share this concern.

On the one hand, you're weighing the total value we bring to the table against a cheaper price. Which of these two alternatives poses the greater threat: paying a little more than you anticipated on the front end, or not receiving everything you need on the back end?

Let's talk again before you make the final decision.

Regards,
Thomas P. Reilly

P.S. I've attached a list of ten things to consider about our package.

Sales Letter 17: Value-Added Services

When you want to emphasize specific value-added services during the pursuit mode, this "ten-things-to-consider" letter carries the load.

Dear Customer/Prospect:

Thanks for the opportunity to discuss our value-added solution. From our meeting, I've put together a list of ideas on how we bring value to you.

[List ten value-added extras here numbered 1–10]

[Customer's name], I feel we've established some great momentum. Let's keep the ball rolling.

Sincerely,
Thomas P. Reilly

P.S. What impact will these value-added services have on your company?

Sales Letter 18: Special Occasion

Whether it's a birthday, an anniversary, or some other special event, a little recognition goes a long way toward building the relationship with the customer.

Dear Customer/Prospect:

We congratulate you on your recent promotion to senior vice president at Coal Industries. This new position presents challenges that will prove your fifteen years of experience quite valuable. I'm confident you will meet those challenges—and then some!

We hope you'll keep us as an integral part of your future plans. Best wishes to you for a successful career advancement.

Sincerely,
Thomas P. Reilly

P.S. [Insert P.S. here]

Sales Letter 19: Holiday Greetings

Use this letter for special holidays throughout the year to let customers know you're thinking of them.

Dear Customer:

During this time of the year we like to reflect on our many blessings and the folks who make them happen. Naturally you're at the top of the list.

Just in case I don't say it enough—thanks for everything you do for us.

Sincerely,
Thomas P. Reilly

P.S. [Insert P.S. here]

Sales Letter 20: Sharing Information

When you run across information that you would like to share with your customers, use this text.

Dear Customer/Prospect:

I thought about you recently when I came across the enclosed article. It occurred to me that you might find this interesting reading.

As always, it's a pleasure working with you.

Sincerely,
Thomas P. Reilly

P.S. [Insert P.S. here]

Sales Letter 21: Apology

There are times when you must belly up to the bar and apologize for something to a customer. It's a great opportunity to show your character.

Dear Customer:

I understand what you're feeling and I believe you have a right to feel this way. We dropped the ball, and there's no excuse—just an explanation.

This experience has strengthened our resolve to fix these types of problems so we never have to inconvenience you again.

Please accept my sincere apology for the problems this mishap caused you. Also, I want to express my gratitude for your willingness to grant us some understanding on this issue. We want to serve you well.

Sincerely,
Thomas P. Reilly

P.S. [Insert P.S. here]

Sales Letter 22: Value Reminder

There are times when you want to send letters that will remind customers of your going the extra mile. It reinforces your position of value with the customer.

Dear Customer:

Just a brief note to follow up on the joint calls I made with your sales reps last week. We uncovered three promising opportunities for your company.

Amherst Coal looks as if it may purchase $15,000 from us over the next year.

General Cable expressed interest in our extended maintenance agreements ($4,500 this year).

Fairfax Steel liked our new processing modules. This is a long-term opportunity—maybe $100,000 or more!

It's great what we can accomplish together, isn't it?

Best regards,
Thomas P. Reilly

P.S. When do you want to celebrate?

Value-Added Selling Review and Action Points

1. Sales letters offer you the opportunity to stand out from the crowd, because so few salespeople use them effectively. Every sales letter you send is another marketing exposure with the prospect or customer.
2. Asking yourself specific organizational questions before composing sales letters will help you design a more effective letter: Who is the reader? And what is my objective?

3. Speak directly to the reader, keep it simple, and remember that less is more. Vary the tone of your letter to reflect the personality of your buyer. Before you send the sales letter, read and edit the letter. You want to put your best foot forward. Make this letter your best work.

CHAPTER 26

VALUE-ADDED TIME MANAGEMENT

FINALLY, UNDERSTANDING AND living the value-added philosophy must include a look at our most precious and fleeting resource—time. We never have enough of it, yet we have all there is. This is the time management paradox. Time is something I feel passionately about. It's my commodity. I sell it.

Success in any profession depends on how well one manages time. I've never met a disorganized successful person. Have you?

At the beginning of my three-day Value-Added Selling seminars, I ask salespeople this question: "What would you like to gain from this program?" "Time management" ranks at the top of their priorities list, equal to "closing more sales." Salespeople understand the importance of managing their time and territories effectively.

Being a better time manager means increased productivity and greater effectiveness. As a better time manager, you are able to protect your off time and guard against the stress that comes from urgency. As a better time manager, you feel more confident and in control.

This chapter helps you manage yourself and your territory more effectively. Specifically, I cover the following topics:

- How salespeople use and misuse time
- Time management myths and realities
- The attitudes of effective management
- How to become more effective and efficient in the way you use your time

- How to plan your week
- How to manage your pipeline of opportunities

How Salespeople Use Time

According to *Sales and Marketing Management Magazine*, salespeople spend less than one-third of their time in face-to-face selling. They spend the balance on "administrivia" such as paperwork, meetings, servicing, waiting, and traveling. In real time, this means that salespeople are in front of customers only one and one-half days per week. Twenty years ago, a McGraw-Hill study found that salespeople spent 40 percent of their day (two full days per week) in face-to-face selling. These numbers represent a disturbing downward trend.

Some people may argue that the advent of E-mail, beepers, fax machines, and cell phones enables salespeople to spend less time in front of customers. Those who hold this position maintain that technology is part of the problem, yet that's not what my research shows. My conclusion is that there are too many distractions for salespeople today.

I have surveyed salespeople over the years to determine their primary time wasters. The top four time wasters, in order of frequency, represent 78 percent of the ways in which salespeople waste their time:

- Attempting to do too much
- Getting distracted by interruptions
- Crisis management—putting out fires
- Administrivia—paperwork, busywork

Do you notice a pattern? All time management problems and solutions can be broken down into one of two categories: efficiency and effectiveness. Efficiency is doing things the right way. Effectiveness is doing the right things. The top four time wasters for salespeople relate to effectiveness. They are primarily problems with setting priorities and remaining on point.

Attempting to do too much means that you have difficulty setting priorities. The same is true for crisis management and administrivia. Crisis management is working on someone else's priorities, not yours. Have you noticed that most of your urgent tasks are someone else's top priorities? Administrivia, by its own definition, is a lower-priority task. Dealing with interruptions is a focus issue. It means you have trouble staying with goal-oriented behavior and eliminating distractions along the way. If you can eliminate most or all of these top four time wasters, you would immediately become more effective.

The goal of time management is to structure one's environment and activities to live a balanced life and to work effectively and efficiently. Successful salespeople are organized, not agonized. They make it a habit to do what others consider to be a hassle. They understand that good time management is habit substitution. They will substitute an effective and efficient way of doing something for an ineffective or inefficient way of doing something. They know that good time management is good self-management. They cannot really manage time—they manage their behavior within the constraints of time. They believe that good time management is consistent, not intermittent. They act on purpose, with purpose.

There is a key word in the previous paragraph: *balanced*. Any definition of time management that excludes balanced living is unrealistic and unhealthy. Becoming more effective in managing your time leads to greater balance in your personal life. Time management is not just about getting more done on the job; it's also about enjoying your whole life more fully.

How successful are you when you find ways to stay at the office longer and away from your home and family more often? I would argue that you need time management more desperately than others if you're spending too much time on the job.

One-dimensional living is a path of self-destruction. Do you know people who have only work going for them? How boring. Do you know people who are so self-centered and "me-deep" in conversation that they believe the world was created just for them? How boorish. Have you ever been in the giving mode to the degree that you attended to everyone's needs except your own? At some point, you begin to resent everyone and everything that puts more demands on your time. These demands are the net result of unbalanced living. Good time management must include good life management.

A few years ago, I discovered some statistics that showed how much time vacationers spend performing work-related activities. The most conservative estimate was that 25 percent of people spent some vacation time doing work or checking in with the boss. A more liberal estimate was 40 percent. I believe that both of these numbers are low by today's standards. Laptop computers now give us a chance to check E-mail and get work done while we're away from the office. Voice mail is a way to check in with the office without really checking in. And some bosses even require employees to call in a couple of times during vacation. Why do you want to take your boss on vacation with you? The purpose of a vacation is to relax and recharge. How can you do that if you never really get away from it all?

Time Management Myths and Realities

After twenty years of sales training experience and having trained more than 100,000 salespeople, I've heard some amazing opinions about time management—excuses, explanations for time wasters, myths, semi-truths, and so on. In this section, I explore some of the myths and realities of time.

Myth 1: I Must Work Hard to Be Successful

This is a variation of another myth: "Being busy is being productive." Many salespeople believe that they are paid to make calls, not sales. To some, it's a shock when I point out that they are paid to create results.

Another variation of this being-busy myth is that the best way to start your day is to get the easy stuff out of the way first and then do the tough stuff. Another school of thought says that you should get the tough stuff done first, and the rest of the day will be a breeze.

Here's reality: There's a bit of truth to both schools of thought. Successful people work hard and smart. Hard work alone is not enough; you must work smart. You can make the best sales presentation of your career, but if it's on the wrong prospect, you've wasted your time. You can work diligently on a project, but what if it's a low-priority task that distracts you from more important duties? All you've proved is that you're a hard worker, not a smart worker. Successful salespeople work hard and smart. They act on purpose, with purpose.

To quote my friend and fellow professional speaker Bill Brooks, "The shoulder-to-the-wheel-and-nose-to-the-grindstone philosophies make sense if you work smart. Otherwise, you end up with tired, aching shoulders and a raw, bloody nose."

Myth 2: Some People Seem to Have More Time than Others

Of all dynamics of success, time is the most democratic. You have all there is. No one has any more than you. There is no more time available. Time is the most level playing field in business. Everyone has all there is, but no one seems to have enough. Sound familiar? The real issue is how well you use what you have. Why are some people able to accomplish more than others in the same time period? It's how they use their time. They make it a habit to work on important matters—high-payoff activities that move them closer to achieving their goals.

Your effectiveness hinges on how well you choose to use this fixed commodity, time. Then your attention must turn to how you determine your priorities. You have a fixed amount of time to accomplish things. Shouldn't you fill those days with high-payoff activities?

Myth 3: The Only Productive Use of My Sales Time Is Face-to-Face with Customers

Now I'm really going to confuse you: Wrong! This myth is a close relative to the being-busy myth. There are effective uses of your time aside from your being in front of a customer. A more relevant question to ask is this: "What are you doing when you're not in front of the customer?" Perhaps you're researching for the customer, designing a proposal for an important piece of business, or solving a problem that will regain lost business. You may be attending a sales training seminar to help you sell at higher margins. All are great uses of your time!

Planning and preparing for a sales call will increase the probability of your success. Rehearsing for a group presentation is an important part of the sales process. Depending on the nature of the activity, some sales activities may be limited to prime selling hours, while others can be done anytime.

Myth 4: It's My Customer, and I Must Do Everything for This Customer Myself

I admire your commitment to service. However, does your customer really want you personally to do everything for him or her, or does the customer want results. For example, if there is an invoice problem, does your customer want you to retype the invoice yourself or to get it fixed? Does a customer who wants a rush shipment expect you to deliver it personally or to make sure that it is handled properly? Customers want results. They are less concerned with who does it.

This fourth myth is an extension of the attitude that says, "It's just easier to do it myself." This stance may result from a lack of trust in others in your organization. Or it could be that you're too possessive when it comes to your customers: "It's my customer, and I must serve my customer." This attitude is self-defeating, because you should want others in your company to share responsibility for customer satisfaction. That won't happen if you demonstrate territoriality regarding your customers.

Myth 5: Every Customer Deserves the Same Amount of Time

Again, your heart is in the right place. Nevertheless, not every customer wants or deserves the same amount of time and effort as your top accounts. Not all business is good business. In Chapter 5, "Value-Added

Target Account Selection," I elaborated on this concept and offered you guidelines for setting account priorities. Every account is different and requires a different level of attention. Beware of low-margin, high-aggravation customers. The time you spend with them may limit your ability to call on more profitable accounts.

Myth 6: It Takes Too Much Time to Plan

Over the years, I've heard variations of this myth: "I'm spontaneous. I go with the flow." "I don't want to limit myself by writing down my goals." "My week is too chaotic to plan." "I must look for whichever fire is burning the brightest, and that's how I set priorities." "I just can't do it" (manage my time, that is).

This last statement presents another time management paradox: You can't do it, but you must do it. It reminds me of the sales manager who asked me to speak at one of his sales meetings. The topic was time management. He knew that his salespeople had to do it but told me they were too busy to do it. I said, "That's exactly why you should do this now. If you can't find the time for a time management seminar, your folks really need to hear this message." He agreed, reluctantly but laughingly.

The people who tell me they are too busy or too spontaneous for traditional time management are really saying they want help but don't want to hear traditional time management tips because these tips do not work for them. If you fit this profile, there is hope. Everyone has his or her own style and unique personality. Regardless of your personality or time management style, value-added time management can and will work for you. Fundamentally, do the tasks you perform daily add value to your efforts? If not, you're working on the wrong stuff.

Whether you use a standard organizer, a palm device, a laptop program, or index cards, your style can work for you. The goal is not to use one particular system. The point is to have a system that helps you set priorities and remain fixed on these priorities. If you can do it with a yellow pad and red marker, go for it. If you need a $200 leather binder to stay organized, buy it. If you like to play with technology and want to organize electronically, more power to you.

Time Management Attitudes

Earlier in this book, I introduced you to the concept that attitude drives behavior. Time management is one of the areas in which attitude plays a central role in your effectiveness. Now it's time to look at several positive time management attitudes that will help you to become more effective.

Gifts of Time

Do you have the gifts-of-time attitude? The gifts-of-time attitude recognizes that ordinary, everyday life hands you moments of time to be either used well or wasted. Your attitude toward these moments determines your stress level. Let's say you're in the express line at the grocery store, and the person in front of you has two extra items in his basket that push him over the ten-item limit. How do you handle this situation?

Some people, I call them the shopping-line police, feel the need to call attention to the ten-item limit. They say something to the "offender." This causes stress, and it adds no value to the interaction. Someone who has the gifts-of-time attitude will view this unexpected delay as serendipity—a pleasant surprise. This person may use the unexpected gift of time to catch up on reading the point-of-sale magazines. Another person may see this break as an opportunity to meet a new friend and strike up a conversation with another person in line. Still another person may perceive it as a chance to spend a few minutes with his or her Creator. These positive reactions add value to each person's days.

Your attitude toward time, especially toward these gifts of time, determines the stress level at which you choose to operate. How effectively can you use your time when you feel stress? Do you have the gifts-of-time attitude? Is time your friend or foe? Does your attitude toward time add value or add stress to your day?

Waiting is an attitude. When a customer keeps you waiting for ten or twenty minutes, how do you use that time? Some salespeople will sit and stew. Others use that time to prepare and review their notes again. It's a gift of time. It's similar to the student who has studied for a test, and the teacher announces that there will be a twenty-minute delay before the test begins, so the class may use the extra time any way that suits. Serious students will spend this last gift of time reviewing what they already know.

Respect

Do you respect time? Value-added salespeople respect time—their own as well as other people's. When you respect your time, you automatically send out signals to others, and they, too, will respect your time. A healthy respect for your time means that you will make the best use of it. By respecting others' time, you acknowledge that their time is as important to them as your time is to you.

Demonstrating respect for time is especially important in sales. In Chapter 23, I pointed out that high-level decision makers use time as a weapon. They appreciate the significance of having so many dreams and so little time. For them, time is a precious commodity. You establish credibility with them by mirroring their respect for time.

Be cautious of spending time with customers who have nothing *but* time. These people ramble and meander incessantly. They are spending your most precious resource at your expense. If people have that much time on their hands, aren't you the least bit curious as to why? Maybe they have nothing else going on. Beware of those who have nothing but time.

Assertiveness

Be assertive with your time. You alone are responsible for how you use your time. No one is more responsible than you for protecting your time. Not your boss. Not your spouse. Not your assistant. You are the most accountable and responsible guardian of your time.

Assertiveness and respect go hand in glove. If you respect your time, you will assert yourself when it comes to others who misuse your time. If you have difficulty asserting yourself, begin by working on respect for your time. Learn how to say no to people and projects. The world is filled with people who will use your time as a way to get more time for themselves. Some go to great lengths to manipulate others into doing things for them that they should do for themselves.

You cannot please everyone. In fact, there is an emotional disorder reserved for those who try. It's called the please-me syndrome. If you try to please everyone, you generally end up pleasing few—especially yourself. As you attempt to serve others selflessly and tirelessly—an admirable quality—and work on their priorities versus your priorities, you may help them get their work done but fail to complete your work in the process.

I understand the importance of teamwork, and I value it. I also am leery of people who make it a habit of finding ways to enlist the aid of others to do their work. Your ability to sift through requests and identify legitimate requests to help others will automatically eliminate one of the biggest time wasters all people experience: interruptions.

At this point, you are probably thinking, "Boy, this guy Reilly is ruthless when it comes to time." You're right! I am. And I hope to share some of this attitude and respect for time with you. Until you develop a similar ruthlessness, you will never have enough time to accomplish your goals. Until you develop the habit of prudently saying no to others' requests, projects, and priorities, you will spend more time working on their objectives than your own. Successful people respect their time and others' time and are far more sensitive and accepting of the need for you to respectfully decline their requests. At a gut level, they understand the importance of time.

Control

You must control your time! Do you run your territory, or does your territory run you? Do you attack your day, or does your day attack you? Are you in control of how you use your time? Most of what happens to you is something over which you have control. Most of what happens is the result of choice, not chance. You make decisions about the behaviors in which you engage. Successful time managers control their days as much as possible. They live the philosophy "If it is to be, it's up to me."

Unsuccessful time managers go through their days by accident. Being in control of your time means starting the day with this question: "What do I want to accomplish today?" Being out of control means beginning your day with the attitude "OK, phone: ring. Tell me, world: what am I supposed to do today?"

There are things you control in your life and things over which you have little or no control. A simple rule of thumb is to spend time and energy on something in proportion to the amount of control you have over that something. Those things over which you have maximum control demand more focus and energy on your part. Things over which you have minimal or no control deserve less focus and energy. Time management is something over which you have significant control. You have a choice as to how you want to invest your time during the day. You can invest it in goal-achieving activities or squander it on nonproductive tasks. It is your choice.

Proactive Versus Reactive

Be proactive in how you invest your time. Proactive time managers anticipate. They are forward thinkers who take the initiative and act. Reactive time managers have a wait-and-see attitude. They live life a day at a time. They specialize in responding, as opposed to initiating. A proactive approach to time management is goal achieving. A reactive approach is more crisis relieving. Proactive time managers control their days. Reactive time managers relinquish some control to their days. Proactive time managers prevent fires. Reactive time managers fight fires.

Ask yourself this fundamental question daily to adopt a more proactive attitude toward time management: "What can I do today to stay ahead of the game?" This shifts your focus to the future. It encourages you to plan and take initiative. By being proactive, you ensure that you are working on your priorities versus someone else's priorities. You are staging activities that keep you on the path of goal achievement. You are running your day instead of letting your day run you.

Becoming More Effective

Effectiveness is working on the right stuff. It begins with knowing what's most important to you, remaining directed toward that goal, and scheduling weekly and daily priorities that move you closer to where you want to be. This is focus and the power of discernment.

Effectiveness means concentrating your energy with laserlike intensity in areas that will yield the return you desire. It's the dynamic less-is-more philosophy. It's going an inch wide and a mile deep. It's locking in on your goals and locking out the distractions along the way. I call this the *discipline of effort*. It's your stick-to-itiveness. Focus is positive tunnel vision.

Focus begins with knowing what's important to you. Most people begin the process by setting goals, but focus is more fundamental than that. It's knowing why you want what you want, which forms your mission, your guiding principle, your vision, your purpose, and your dream. It's what you value most in this world. Focus cuts to the core of your motivation. It's what you are willing to give your life for—because you do.

Some years ago, I met a financial planner who asked me about my long-term goals. I said that I wanted to retire at age forty-five. She pressed me with, "Why?" but I didn't have a good answer for her. Her question haunted me until, one day, the lightbulb went on, and the answer occurred to me. Retirement for me was total financial independence. More fundamental was the insight that what motivates me more than money is personal independence. I value autonomy. I like calling my own shots and being on my own. Eureka! Since I was self-employed at the time, I was already living the dream of independence. My goals shifted immediately.

Before you set goals and begin focusing on them, ask yourself why those goals are important to you. This insight into your motivation will help you realign your goals to make them more consistent with what you really want from life. Once you've discovered that, you're focused. Then, you can begin to set priorities.

The power of discernment is knowing what to work on and, more important, what not to work on. It is establishing priorities that help you get more of what you want from life. How do you think most people set priorities? If you said, "By urgency," you would be correct. Most folks set priorities by determining which fire is burning the brightest and attending to it. How does urgency make you feel: Stressed? Pressured? Exhausted? Excited?

How does it feel when you set priorities by payoff? You feel confident and in control. You're working on goal-achieving activities that move you closer to what you want from life. When you set priorities by urgency, you're generally working on someone else's high priorities.

Figure 26.1 offers a graphic representation. If you set priorities by payoff (Q1 and Q2, for example), you are engaging in goal-achieving behavior. If you set priorities by urgency (Q1 and Q3), you are engaging in crisis-relieving behavior.

Here are some questions to ask yourself to help you set priorities more effectively:

- Does this activity really add value to my day?
- What is the return on my time investment?
- What trade-offs am I making by doing this activity?
- Does this activity keep me on the path to my goals?
- Is this task goal achieving or crisis relieving?

The most direct route to becoming more effective is to invest more time in areas that produce the results you want and less time on the

Figure 26.1 Effective matrix

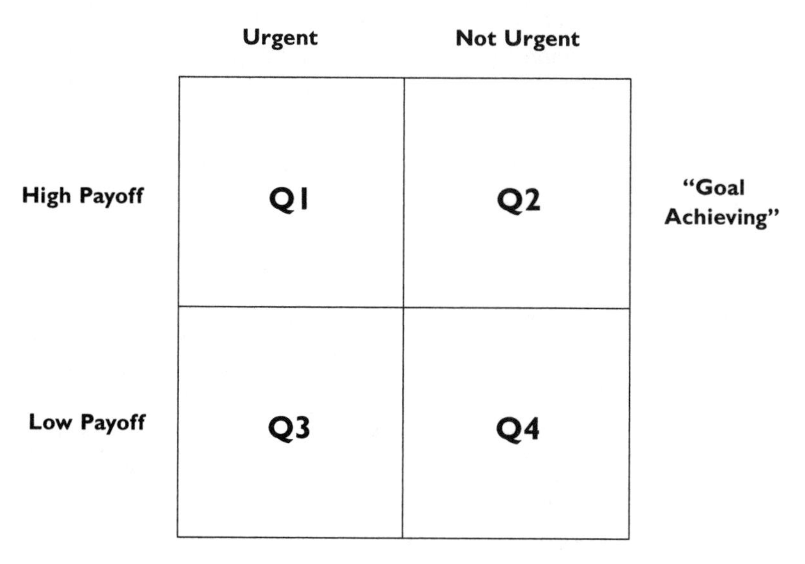

"noise" along the way. Is it noise, or is it necessary? Everyone has a certain amount of clutter on his or her radar screen. Your objective is to separate the clutter from the mission-critical activities and to keep your sights trained on these mission-critical, goal-achieving activities. It requires discipline, respect for your time, and the assertiveness to say no to the distractions around you. Minimize the grunt work, and maximize the producer work.

Becoming More Efficient

Efficiency is doing things the right way: time compression and expansion. Compression is streamlining, eliminating time wasters, and trimming the fat from your day. Many people keep time logs to determine which activities add value to their days and which activities are a drain to their days. The first serious time log I kept spanned three weeks. I kept a legal pad next to my phone and wrote down everything I did during this three-week period. I was shocked to discover that I spent ten hours per week during working hours on personal matters—stopping by the mall because of a shirt sale, talking to friends on the phone, and so forth. This made me painfully aware of how I needed to practice what I preached—or, in my business, walk the talk.

Another compression tip is bunching, batching, or grouping. Here, you perform related tasks at the same time because you have all the tools at your disposal and the mind-set to work on these tasks. For instance, you may complete several expense reports in succession because you're in that frame of mind. You can do your account planning for key accounts at one sitting. If you need to visit your office during business hours, you may want to talk to all the inside folks with whom you have business while you're there. Returning all of your phone calls in one time block is another example.

Streamlining includes handling each piece only once when you sort your mail. If a piece of mail requires an acknowledgment on your part, write a note on the paper itself, and send it on its way. If it's an FYI, read it, file it, or dump it. Read mail with your trash can at your side. Scan a magazine's table of contents for interesting articles. If nothing interests you, pitch the magazine, or pass it along. Attend only parts of meetings that are relevant to you. Do you need to be there for the whole thing?

Travel efficiently. What is the most direct route? How can you avoid traffic? Do you really need to make this call in person, or can you handle the transaction by phone or E-mail? When you travel to remote areas, do you need to visit all accounts in that area, or can you spend your time better back at the motel, making phone calls to other viable prospects?

To become more efficient, practice the habit of pursuing excellence, not perfection. Pursuing excellence means you do the best job you can with the resources you have available. Waiting for perfection is a form of procrastination. Some things do not require perfection. Brain surgery? Yes. Cleaning out your desk drawers? No.

Expand your time with the principle of leverage—one of the eleven Value-Added Selling strategies I discussed in Part II. Multiply your efforts by enlisting the aid of other people to sell for you inside your accounts. These are your internal champions. Successful people understand the importance of delegation. The question is not "Will I delegate?" The question is "To whom will I delegate?" To others, or to yourself by default?

Cross-sell related products and services. Use all the tools and technology at your fingertips to help you achieve a higher ratio of return on your time investment. Leveraging is attaining twelve hours of productivity from an eight-hour day. It's gaining 150 percent return from 100 percent effort.

Planning

Planning is dreaming on paper. Specifically, it's your link between dreams and reality. Planning is shaping and creating your future in your mind first, and then on paper. It's scheduling focused priorities that will serve as a catalyst to moving you closer to achieving your goals. Few salespeople have a systematic way of planning their weeks and days. The following principles will help you get more from your planning.

- ***Develop a routine so that it becomes a habit for you.*** Planning will be an integral part of your weekly ritual. Some people like to plan the Friday before, and others like to plan first thing Monday morning. When you plan is up to you. Plan when it best fits your schedule and personality. You may need to plan first thing Monday morning to get you started. Fine. But do it.
- ***Stretch your time horizon.*** Daily planning is OK if you're going through life a day at a time. At a minimum, plan weekly. Monthly planning is better. When you stretch your planning time horizon, you're focusing on a common theme for the month, quarter, or year. You don't micro-focus on minutia. What is the most important way for you to use your time this month? What do you want your focus to be this quarter? What is your overall goal for the year?
- ***Schedule your priorities.*** Ask yourself, "What do I want to accomplish this week?" The opposite question to avoid is "What do I have to get done?" The first is proactive, and the latter is reactive. Schedule high-payoff, mission-critical activities that move you closer to your goals. Review these goals as part of your weekly planning ritual to keep yourself mission focused.
- ***Consider your peak times when planning.*** Are you an owl or a lark? My creative time of the day is early morning, and that's when I do all of my writing. If you're an afternoon person, you should schedule more challenging events during this peak time for you. Play at the top of your game. Schedule time for regeneration—physical and mental. Have a plan for professional study. Leave time in your schedule to relax.
- ***Plan for balance.*** Consider all the main areas of your life, and attend to each area weekly and daily: work, home, personal, spiritual, financial, self-development, and social.
- ***Schedule prudently.*** Be available to others, and make time for yourself. Consider your main functional areas in your job, and schedule time for each one. If you're evaluated on customer retention, plan to spend time with existing customers to assure their satisfaction. If you're evaluated on landing new business, plan time to pursue new business.
- ***Schedule realistically.*** To maintain your sanity and a reasonable workload, take a tip from a friend of mine who happens to be one of

the gurus of time management, Dr. Larry Baker: Schedule about half of your day, to allow for interruptions and distractions. Adjust up or down depending on your job and your schedule.

- ***Create a checklist.*** Keeping a list of your mission-critical activities keeps you focused on your goals. Review the list weekly. I call this my Weekly Checklist, and I've used this concept for years. Here's a sample of what's on my list:
  - Review goals
  - Review marketing plan
  - Scan calendar for the next month to see what projects I want to work on
  - Check sales numbers for past month and project forward three months
  - Complete last week's expense reports
  - Check business-pending file and schedule action items
  - Prepare for this week's seminars
  - Follow up on last week's seminars

This routine takes me about fifteen minutes each week, and it keeps me focused on the goals I want to accomplish and other details that keep my business running smoothly. Faithfully using my Weekly Checklist means I find that few things ever slip by me. I keep this list in my personal organizer, and I have created a weekly planning form that parallels the major functional areas of my job.

Planning is a habit, just like not planning. Time management is really habit substitution. You're substituting one habit for another. Adopt the planning habit. Value-added salespeople make it a habit to do those things others can't or won't do. How many times have I said this? This is an opportunity area. If others dislike doing it and you embrace the habit, you have distanced yourself from the rest of the crowd.

Opportunities Management

Opportunities management has been one of the most fascinating and dynamic areas of time management over the years. We used to call it managing your pipeline, time and territory management, and establishing a tickler file. Today, opportunities management is the name most trainers and managers use to describe what salespeople must do to attend to all the business opportunities in their pipelines. If you were to conceive of a model that includes suspects, prospects, and red-hot prospects, you could manage these different opportunities more effectively.

Suspects are leads—either existing customers or noncustomers. You have some reason to believe they may represent an opportunity for you. You might have read an article about a company moving into your area, or your boss might have passed along a lead to you, saying, "Follow up on this." Maybe your company has launched a new product line, and you have a list of accounts from your existing base that you feel are viable targets for this new line. Suspects remain in this position of the pipeline as a single, qualifying contact. If they appear to be a viable opportunity, they move through your pipeline to the next status, prospects.

Prospects are qualified leads. There is a reasonable possibility that you will do business with them. This is where the bottleneck generally occurs in sales, because of the amount of time you spend following up on these prospects. If you spend too much time in this mode, these prospects turn into "prisoner-of-hope" accounts. Everyone has these. There are always business opportunities that salespeople pursue because their optimism and persistence will not allow them to quit. At some point, you know you have become a prisoner of hope, and you must change your strategy. Modify your call frequency and follow-up. Spend less time on these prisoner-of-hope accounts, which frees up time to invest with viable suspects in the beginning of your pipeline.

Red-hot prospects are the accounts that you feel are close to ordering. Your sales instincts tell you that it's more a matter of when you'll do business than if you'll do business with these accounts. You're about 90 percent sure that you have the business. Your strategy is to live with this account until you get the business. These accounts are the most important opportunities in your pipeline because you are so close to writing the order.

To manage your pipeline effectively and to maintain a solid balance of opportunities, use this ratio: For every red-hot prospect, you need two prospects and four suspects. This 4-2-1 ratio will balance your pipeline with a steady flow of new opportunities.

Value-Added Selling Review and Action Points

1. The two main time wasters for salespeople are failing to set high-payoff priorities and failing to remain focused on high-priority activities. Avoid these two time wasters and you will eliminate 78 percent of the ways your peers waste time.
2. Your attitude about time determines your stress level. To reduce stress, do more of less. As you respect your time, others will also respect it. You alone are responsible for your time.
3. To increase your effectiveness, set priorities by payoff, not urgency. Seek to do more of that which adds value to your life and less of that which adds little or no value to your life.
4. Planning is dreaming on paper. No one plans to fail, but many fail to plan. Begin each week and every day with a few minutes of thoughtful planning. It is your link between dreams and reality.

CHAPTER 27

FINAL THOUGHTS

WHEW! I CAN almost hear you asking, "Where do I go from here?" As I pointed out earlier in this book, Value-Added Selling is a content-rich message of hope. And there's plenty of both—hope and content. Another way to ask this question is, "How do I get the most value from this book and my study of Value-Added Selling?" A book this size and with this much content can be overwhelming when you want to apply what you've learned.

As people complete our Value-Added Selling seminars, they, too, want to apply what they have learned, but they want it to sound like them, not me. And that is great advice. For a smoother transfer of skills, you must internalize the Value-Added Selling themes coursing through the preceding twenty-six chapters and apply them strategically, tactically, and personally, using the models provided. In short, use the ideas here, but make them sound like you.

In this final chapter, I review the fundamental themes of the value-added philosophy and the strategies and tactics of Value-Added Selling. I also offer some follow-up tips for using this material. I want to help you develop an action plan to implement the Value-Added Selling process and get maximum value from your time and money investment.

The value-added philosophy can be reduced to two fundamental concepts. First: *Life is bigger than me*. This fundamental belief in our being a part of something bigger and better than ourselves paves the way for what I call *empowering humility*. This dynamic makes us willingly subordinate our egos for the greater good of serving others—

to embrace the attitude that *serving is a privilege, not a pain.* Implicit in this belief is that we all matter, that we all are important, that what we do matters, and that our work is important—to someone.

This selfless attitude of service does not mean that we ignore our interests; in fact, the opposite is true. We pursue equity in our relationships with customers. We want them to *get* as good as they *give.* The outcome of our sales efforts must be mutually rewarding—the win-win outcome. If it's not a good deal for both parties—buyer and seller—it's not a good deal for either party. We pursue results that benefit the customer and us.

Subordinating one's ego makes it easier to view life from another's perspective, to see life from the other's vantage point, to understand what is important to this person. This bird's-eye view from the customer's perspective makes it easier to find win-win outcomes. Earlier I called this a customer value focus, but the notion of putting someone else's interests first is more fundamental than that.

It also means that we realize that Value-Added Selling is a team sport: *we* is greater than *me.* This synergy recognizes that salespeople may get the business initially, but it is the customer's total experience with a company that determines repeat business. This we-is-greater-than-me philosophy mandates that we treat each other with the same respect that we would hope our best customers receive. We must build each other up, not break each other down.

Humility is at the heart of growth. For any of us to grow, we must first be willing to admit that we are *not there,* yet. It's important for all of us to be proud of our accomplishments, but pride without humility is arrogance. This is empowering humility—it encourages us to grow. We're proud of the past and excited about the future.

Second: *My mission is to add value, not cost.* From this grows the following attitude: "Do more of that which adds value to your life and less of that which adds little or no value." This attitude applies to all areas of your life—health, relationships, time management, career, and spiritual and emotional well-being. When you're in the value-added mode, you're part of the momentum of life, not the resistance of life. In aeronautical terms, you're part of the thrust, not part of the drag. You're pulling the wagon versus being part of the load.

Adding value depends on your initiative and curiosity. Implicit in this concept and concomitant with empowering humility is your belief that you can make something better, that you can add more value. As a value-added salesperson, you possess the initiative to act on this belief. Your destiny is to grow and to develop, and to contribute more of that which adds value. Because of your customer value focus, you seek to add value that is meaningful to customers, not just sellers.

Empowering humility, a restless curiosity about your potential, and the burning initiative to act encourage you to pursue excellence in all that you do. Do less than that and you cheat yourself out of your destiny to become a value-added peak competitor and deny the customer the best you have to offer.

Preparation

Preparation encompasses both personal and collateral preparation. Personal preparation is continuous investment in your own research and development. Study. Invest in your knowledge base. Increase your personal brand equity for the customer. Become an expert in your field. You want to become the standard against which all other salespeople are compared. Value-added salespeople are serious students of our profession. After you have garnered all that you want to take from this book, buy another book on sales. Read and apply what you learn in that book. Enroll in seminars. Sign up for company product training sessions. Attend factory schools. Seventy-six percent of the value added that buyers receive comes from knowledge-based activities.

Collateral preparation means that you need sales tools to help you persuade the buyer of your value-added solution. Create your VIP list on company letterhead. Study this value added. To sell your value added, you must know your value added. Design a Customer's Bill of Rights and use it to convince buyers that you're serious about serving. Value-added work sheets will help you "tangible-ize" your value added for customers. Prepare a list of rebuttals for price objections, and commit them to memory. Work on your proposal format. Use the sales letters in this book. Design no-charge invoices to remind the customer of your value added. All of these tools will support you in your efforts to present compelling reasons for customers to buy your alternatives.

Strategic Prescriptions

The ideal scenario for you is to have a sales coach with you all of the time, offering suggestions and guidance on your efforts. In most cases, that's not practical, so you must become your own sales coach. The following coaching questions review the strategic side of Value-Added Selling while directing you to apply them tactically in your territory on an account-by-account basis. Ask yourself these questions to remain focused on the Value-Added Selling philosophy and process:

- Am I chasing the right business? Is this a value-added target account?
- Am I talking to all the right people? Am I getting full and deep account penetration?
- Do I really know how my customers think? Do I understand what they need, want, and fear? Do I know their organizational and personal issues?
- What image have I created in the buyer's mind about our products, our company, and myself?
- Have I differentiated our solution? What are the definable and defendable differences between us and the competition?
- Can I present a compelling reason for the buyer to choose our alternative?
- Am I providing the buyer with a smooth, seamless, and painless transition to our solution?
- How is my relationship with the customer—personally and professionally?
- Am I working as hard to keep this business as I worked initially to get it? Am I seeking ways to re-create value for the customer?
- Are we getting credit for all of the value added we bring to this customer?

- Am I getting all of the business in this account? Are there other sales opportunities I should pursue?

If I were your personal sales coach and I could be with you daily as you make sales calls, I would ask you these questions and more:

- Are you making enough calls?
- How is the quality as well as the quantity of your calls?
- Do you feel you're effective?
- Are you focused?
- Are you setting priorities by payoff or by urgency?
- How much time do you spend in the offensive selling mode and in the defensive selling mode?
- How do you deal with prisoner-of-hope accounts?
- Are you calling on enough high-level decision makers?

Tactical Prescriptions

When you make sales calls, use the tips in this section to direct your calling efforts. Be sure to have a specific objective for every call.

Precall Planning

Prepare for every call by asking these six questions:

- What do I want to accomplish on this call?
- What questions will I ask?
- What will I present to the buyer?
- What collateral pieces do I need?
- What resistance may I encounter?
- At the end of the call, what action do I want from the buyer?

Plan your sales call by using the call planning guide. Ten minutes of pencil-and-paper preparation reaps huge dividends in confidence and competence. My personal success formula is P + P = 2P: Planning and Preparation equals twice the Performance.

During Your Sales Call

- Open the call by telling the buyer why you're there—state your objective.
- Take your lead from the buyer on small talk and socializing.
- Spend the first half of the call probing and listening to the buyer's needs. Ask more open-ended questions than closed-ended questions. Probe deep for "root-canal-type" pain.
- Present relevant sales messages that mirror the buyer's concerns. Include all three dimensions of value in these sales points: product features and benefits, company value-added services, and personal commitments from you, the value-added salesperson.
- Close the sales call by agreeing on your next step to advance the sale along your path. Get some commitment from the buyer that reflects your call objective. Ask for the order.

After the Sales Call

Review every sales call immediately after you make the call, and ask yourself these questions:

- Did I achieve my objectives?
- How was the chemistry between the buyer and me?
- What is the next action step? Schedule it before you leave the parking lot.
- Why was I successful in spite of any obstacles I faced?

This last point is critical to your long-range success. To maintain your success momentum, you must understand what works best for you so that you can go out on your next sales call and do it all over again.

And Finally

Again, thank you for buying this book. I appreciate your faith in the Value-Added Selling philosophy. Congratulations on your reading this book. Your commitment to buying and reading *Value-Added Selling* says a great deal about your commitment to our profession. I'm proud to share that with you. I wish you great continued success.

You can stay abreast of updates for *Value-Added Selling* by visiting this website: valueaddedselling.com. I'll leave you with some words from Thomas Wolfe: "If a man has a talent and cannot use it, he has failed. If he has a talent and uses only half of it, he has partly failed. If he has a talent and learns somehow to use the whole of it, he has gloriously succeeded, and won a satisfaction and a triumph few men ever know." You have the talent; you have the opportunity—the rest is up to you. God bless.

INDEX